For Coralie and Garance

Gilles Roux

Glossary for occasionally snarky managers

240+ terms to survive the business jungle

Aknowledgements

This book would not be in your hands if some friends, and sometimes indirect supporters, had not given their wise opinion, their encouragement, and their corrections.

For this reason, I would like to thank those who, through their commitment, helped me to finish this glossary:

- Clem Mitchell for his patience, his support and his corrections of an originally clumsy text.
- Pascal Koschwitz who read all the definitions with attention and a red pencil. He knew how to bring some intelligence to the primitive form of the first draft.
- Dr. Ingo Zorbach with whom I share a sarcastic sense of humour and who echoed my laughter so many times.
- Nicole Wesley who read this glossary and encouraged me to publish it.

Thanks to all of you.

© 2021 Gilles Roux
Cover, Illustrations: Patrick Tiedtke
Publisher: tredition
ISBN
Paperback   978-3-347-35259-9
Hardcover   978-3-347-35260-5

Table of content

Foreword

Glossaries, dictionaries and telephone directories are not read, they are browsed. They are boring and take up space on the shelves.

So here we are, after 25 years of talking business on five continents with partners from cultures as different as they are far from mine, I decided to write this glossary, which is so decried, but with a snarky note to it.

This glossary lists the words, expressions and quotations that have accompanied my career as a manager of large groups and as an entrepreneur. From time to time, you will find a remark, a wink, or a thought that I hope will make you smile or think back to a similar experience.

Check out this glossary, don't read it like a novel. At the end of each definition or paragraph, you will find a cross-reference after the mention see also. Follow this reference and the next one and the next one. This way you should be able to go through all the definitions like a bee goes from flower to flower.

After the mention opposite, you will sometimes find words (and sometimes thoughts) that are not (fortunately) listed in the glossary.

Finally, you should know that I wrote this glossary for you who have been in the business for years and wanted to remember the meaning of certain terms, for you who are new to the business and are confronted with jargon unknown to the academic, for you who like to speak with the right word, and finally for you who are looking for a glossary that whispers to you and not dictates the word.

I wish you a good read and as much pleasure in reading as I had in writing.

Gilles Roux, in May 2021.

Accountant

The accountant is an essential part of any type of business or professional activity. In charge of keeping the accounts, he or she collects and checks the accounting data, draws up the closing operations and the regulatory documents.

The nature and organisation of an accountant's work varies greatly according to the size of the company and therefore the division of tasks.

There are generally three types of accountant:

— The *accounts receivable* (AR) accountant is responsible for processing and controlling the accounts for sales and collection transactions.
— The *accounts payable* (AP) accountant is specialised in the accounting treatment of purchasing operations and collects supplier invoices from the various departments.
— The *collection* accountant is responsible for recovering the payment of unpaid invoices.

See also: financial statement, order-to-cash, purchase-to-pay

Accountability

Individual accountability is the belief that everyone is accountable for their performance and learning. Individual accountability occurs when each individual's performance is assessed and the results fed back to the team.

Successful teams cannot thrive without accountability in the workplace; results and accountability are inextricably linked. Creating a corporate culture based on accountability is often the secret to successful teams; it fosters better working relationships, improves happiness at work and eliminates surprises.

However, beware of using the word accountability or accountable with non-native speakers of English. In many languages[1], the word is translated as *responsible* or *responsibility*, which can lead to misunderstanding.

opposite: unaccountable
see also: RACI, responsibility

Accretion

Accretion is the continuous increase in a company's profits and assets due to its continuous expansion over a defined timeline. It can result from organic growth or from the acquisition of other entities.

Accretion is also an accounting term that refers to the gain generated by an investor after purchasing a bond at a reduced price. By holding the bond until maturity, the investor gradually realises a profit on the difference between the expected purchase price and the face value of the bond.

« The most successful men in the end are those whose success is the result of steady accretion. » *Alexander Graham Bell*

opposite: decrease
see also: organic growth

Acquisition

Far from being comparable to an impulse purchase in your favourite shopping street, company acquisition is a measured, structured and thoughtful managerial act. It is part of a well thought-out and logical strategic line.

---

[1] e.g. French, German or Spanish

An acquisition is in other words the act of a company taking over another company. To do this, the acquiring company buys the majority or all of the shares of the acquired company.

However, it is unfortunately not uncommon for the size of the acquisition to match the size of the ego of the person making it. In this particular case, it is also not uncommon for the acquisition to become a fiasco.

opposite: disposal
see also: PMI – Post-merger integration

Action plan

An action plan is a of guide that provides a framework or structure when a project is to be carried out.

In a company, an action plan may involve several departments and sectors. The plan establishes who will be responsible for its execution in terms of form and time. It usually also includes a mechanism or some kind of monitoring and control method so that those responsible can analyse whether the steps are on the right track.

The action plan proposes a way to achieve the strategic objectives previously established. It represents the process prior to the actual execution of an idea or proposal.

The action plan turns a goal into objectives. Without an action plan, the goal would be a wish.

opposite: surprise
see also: goal, Knoster's chart, objective

Advantage (competitive)

Competitive advantage is a characteristic that gives a company an upper hand over its rivals. It is something that helps it to be more competitive. A competitive advantage can be a superiority that a company acquires. For example, it may offer better credit terms or a lower price than its competitors.

Some companies with a competitive advantage may charge more. They do this by offering greater added value through differentiation.

opposite: disadvantage
see also: differentiation, value proposition

Advisory Board

An advisory board is an informal group of professionals who can help you better manage your business and formulate your visions, strategy or even thoughts. And since they are not official (they are not regulated by any law), you have a lot of flexibility in how you set them up.

You don't even need to pay them: in other words, they don't have to support you in this case.

see also: director, strategy

Alpha (generation)

The term alpha generation is the brainchild of Australian social scientist Mark McCrindle[2], who used it to refer to people born in the 2010s and beyond. Worthy heirs to Generation Z, they are the first generation that has only ever known the 21st century.

Among the issues they consider most important, keeping children safe at school, making sure everyone has enough to eat, that all people are treated fairly, no matter what they look like and preserving the environment come out on top.

Their way of thinking, seeing and understanding the world and the values they put forward are turning the current socio-economic environment upside down. It would be illusory, if not fatal, not to take into account the needs of this future generation of employees and customers today.

opposite: omega generation (to be born in year 2400)
see also: millennials, X generation, Z generation

Amortisation

Stop thinking that amortisation is the same as depreciation because it is not!

Amortisation is only for intangible assets (items having value, BUT that you can't touch) while depreciation is for tangible assets (items having value, AND that you can touch).

---

[2] Australian social analyst with an international reputation for tracking the emerging trends and analysing the diverse generations.

To add to the confusion, amortization also has a meaning in paying off a debt, like a mortgage, but in the majority of the cases you will face, it has to do with business assets.

see also: depreciation

Artificial Intelligence

Artificial intelligence (AI) is a set of techniques that enable machines to perform tasks and solve problems normally reserved for humans and some animals.

Don't expect me to tell you here about Douglas Adams' depressive robot[3], replacing under- productive employees. Indeed, artificial intelligence has a completely different connotation.

Automatic translators such as Deepl, Facebook's DeepFace facial recognition, Intelligent Character Recognition (ICR), automated customer support in CRMs, chatbots on your company's web page, SPAM detection, targeting of online advertisements according to your behaviour to make money on the Internet, etc.

AI is everywhere in our workplace.

One of the amazing facts about AI-technology is that it loses this name as soon as it becomes useful and becomes part of employees' daily lives. AI is scary, while e.g. interactive software is attractive. That's why the presence of AI in our daily lives doesn't strike us.

From today's business point of view, AI can be defined as a stand-alone computer program capable of learning and giving orders to performers. AI programs "learn" from the data contained in information systems, extract and analyse recurrent patterns, compare them to larger databases, and take decisions somewhat like an automatic pilot. In the future, those programs will advise the users and warn them of any anomalies.

If in 1980, a skill had a duration of about 30 years, from 2021 it will only last a maximum of 5 years. With the deployment of AI, managers will therefore have to reinvent themselves and develop new skills in order to be able to work with artificial intelligence. It will then be a question of collaborative intelligence (men / machines), as it already exists in handling with co-robotics.

opposite: natural stupidity
see also: digitalisation, manager

---

[3] Screenwriter, essayist, humorist, satirist and dramatist. The depressive robot named Marvin, is a protagonist of the bestseller novel: "The Hitchhiker's guide to the Galaxy".

Assets

An asset is an expenditure that has utility through multiple future accounting periods. If an expenditure does not have such utility, it is instead considered an expense.

There are different types of assets: current assets, fixed or non-current assets, tangible assets, intangible assets, operating assets, non-operating assets and the most important if you are getting fired: *You will be an asset for any company you'll go to.*

opposite: liability
see also: expense, investment

Attention

"Paying attention to simple little things that most men neglect makes a few men rich." *Henry Ford[4]*

Attrition rate

The company's attrition rate is the rate at which employees voluntarily leave the company. The attrition rate is also called the turnover rate or *churn* rate. If your company has a high attrition rate, permanent replacement of employees can be costly.

Since employees first leave their boss before leaving the company, it would be wise to consider a change in management when the attrition rate is continuously high: it might be cheaper.

See also: churn rate

Auction (reverse)

A reverse auction literally means the opposite of a traditional auction. In a reverse auction, the objective is to obtain the lowest possible price. Unlike traditional auctions, which are usually held in physical locations, reverse auctions are held online, via a web browser or special software. Despite the fact that this form of auction has killed many companies operating in public markets, it remains a popular form of auction

---

[4] American industrialist, business magnate, and founder of the Ford Motor Company and chief developer of the assembly line technique of mass production.

because of its speed (no negotiation), transparency (all information can be seen by the participants in real time) and - apparently - reduced costs.

opposite: auction
see also: tender

B

Bankruptcy

Bankruptcy is the *insolvency* of states, companies or private individuals, i.e. an economic failure without the possibility of paying off the lenders. In many European countries, the term is defined more narrowly as the intentional or negligent causing of insolvency, which can be punished with imprisonment.

„Capitalism without bankruptcy is like Christianity without hell." *Frank Borman*[5]

see also: insolvency

Benefit (in kind)

Benefits in kind are the provision by an employer of goods or services to employees, either free of charge or in return for a contribution from the employee that is less than the actual value of the service. These benefits thus prevent employees from having to incur expenses. They are common in certain sectors of activity, such as the restaurant and hotel industries, or in certain professions (sales force, sales management).

---

[5] US Air Force colonel, aeronautical engineer, test pilot, businessman, rancher, and NASA astronaut.

Other companies use these benefits to *pamper* and retain their employees, or to attract the best candidates in the market.

see also: compliance, give-away, tax

Blind carbon copy

The abbreviation BCC stands for blind carbon copy. It is a reminder of the days when typewriters were still in use and allowed anyone who hit the keys hard enough to create carbon copies.

The receiver of a BCC mail cannot see who else has received the BCC mail. Similarly, everyone else cannot see who received the mail via BCC either, but the receiver can of course see the CC recipients, the normal recipients and the sender.

In theory, BCC protects the privacy of individual BCC recipients.

In practice, BCC is an interesting if not disturbing aspect of a corporate culture. BCC does not promote transparency in communication nor even trust within the organisation. Many organisations have excluded the possibility of using BCC for this reason and thus be in line with their ethical rules on behaviour towards employees.

opposite: to
see also: carbon copy, ethic, trust

Board (of directors)

A board of directors, also known as the Board or "BoD", is a group of people who have been selected and elected, in a more or less transparent way, by the shareholders of a company to represent their interests.

The board acts as the governing body of a company or corporation. Its main purpose is to protect the shareholders' assets by ensuring that the management of the organisation acts on their behalf and that they get a good return on their investment (ROI) in the company.

What happens at a board meeting is equivalent to what happens in Las Vegas: it stays there.

see also: director, ROI, governance

Branding (corporate)

Corporate branding is the representation of a company (or organisation) as perceived by the consumer. It is also referred to as "branding". Brand messages are conveyed via the Internet, the media and print.

The brand image makes it possible to inform, raise awareness, make people react, and create a link with the customer.

"Brand is just a perception, and perception will match reality over time." *Elon Musk*[6]

see also: branding (employer), reputation, trust

Branding (employer)

Employer branding is the image that a company conveys to its employees and potential candidates through communication and marketing actions in order to make the company attractive.

In other words, the employer brand is everything that makes your employees want to come and work for you on a daily basis and everything that makes candidates want to apply and get a job in your company.

see also: branding (corporate), communication, jobs description

Business

A business is an organisation or entity that sells goods or services for a profit. The important part of this definition is that a business is something that operates in order to make a profit.

Not all businesses actually are successful enough to make a profit, but their main purpose is to generate profits.

In fact, not every activity that keeps you busy is necessarily a business!

see also: the entire glossary

Business angel (angel investor)

This is an investor who is willing to collaborate in an entrepreneurial project. In addition to financial capital, this type of investor may also invest business management know-how or contacts.

Business angels usually have proven experience in business management and in-depth knowledge of a sector of activity.

---

[6] American entrepreneur who cofounded the electronic-payment firm PayPal and formed SpaceX, maker of launch vehicles and spacecraft. He was also one of the first significant investors in, as well as chief executive officer of, the electric car manufacturer Tesla.

These investors not only commit funds to a project, but also time and the power of a network of contacts that can be decisive for the success of the project.

Here are some of the characteristics of the majority of business angels:

- they invest their own funds in the project, unlike venture capitalists whose core business is investing in unlisted companies
- the decision to invest or not is theirs alone,
- they support entrepreneurs with whom they have no family or friendship ties (hence the angelic character!),
- the investment is in principle in solid and viable projects, since business angels often expect a future return,
- the main objective is the profitability of the investment.

see also: love money, start-up

Business card

The business card is a nonsense of economic life in these days of digitalisation. It is a piece of cardboard proudly bearing the logo and name of the prestigious company you represent, your title within it and how to reach you (or your P.A.: which perhaps makes you even more important.)

However, the business card is the indispensable artifact of the ceremonial first physical meeting between two businesspeople. With this piece of cardboard, they can tell their grandchildren: *I met this person!*

see also: *signature*

Business plan

A business plan is a document detailing the company's strategy and financial forecast for the coming years.

This is not a question of whether writing a business plan makes sense or not. There are many examples of global success stories without a business plan, and to deny that the business plan is often not a good match for reality would be pointless.

However, "business plan" is a magic expression used by investors of all kinds and even family members who offer you "love money". It is an obligatory step in the fundraising process.

From a general viewpoint, there are many ways to write a business plan, but there are only 10 ways to screw it up!

1. *Neglecting the form*: form is the number one communication tool and above all the most complex point of failure of all.

2. *Being too technical* : have you solved the perpetual motion or simply created your line of products that everyone is going to be tearing off? Congratulations. But are you sure that all readers want to understand how it works in the jargon you use every day in your laboratory? No. If the investor is interested, then he or she will probably call in an expert during the due diligence.

3. *Information bombing*: the business plan is not a way to put everything you want to say on paper. Remember grandmother's encyclopedia, you would leaf through it but not read it. Well, for investors, it's the same thing! 20-30 pages maximum per business plan, with the right and necessary information.

4. *The market study*: often underestimated, market research is unfortunately often botched. Some limit themselves to a few Google searches and a few online studies on the subject with figures that are often out of date.

5. *The business model*: the business model is the mechanism by which the company generates its profits, while the business plan is a document presenting the company's strategy and expected financial performance for the coming years. The business model, the central part of the business plan, answers the question: how does the money come into my pocket? Easy peasy: Who pays? How much? At what time? Why? All other data in the business plan revolve around the business model.

6. *The assumptions*: the turnover and cost figures can be as complete as possible, it will only make sense if they are accompanied by plausible justifications. An investor or banker will not look at the figures in detail. They will more often prefer the justification of these figures, in other words, the assumptions! Rather than detailing a gigantic spreadsheet in your business plan, give your assumptions and JUSTIFY THEM.

7. *The top-down approach*: adopt a " bottom up " approach to explain the development of the turnover and put it into perspective with the size of the market and the positioning of direct competitors.

8. *The team*: better a wobbly project with an incredible team than the other way around. A great team will always be able to lift

mountains and make things right. In a nutshell: in your business plan, the first product to sell is you!

9. *Customising the business plan*: don't forget that the different readers are destined to be your partners of tomorrow (whether they take an equity stake or lend money). They will therefore have to work together. The language of your business plan must therefore be common to all these parties.

10. *Writing a business plan*: the business plan is great, but don't start with that! Launch a little something to test the market before writing a business plan. Many people who want to perfect the business plan spend too much time on it and fail to timely complete and implement the plan.

"The best business plans are straightforward documents that spell out the who, what, where, why, and how much." *Paula Nelson*[7]

opposite: driving blind
see also: vision, strategy

---

[7] Not the country-music singer but the Paula Nelson, Principal at Nelson Group plc., commentator at CNN Today and bestseller author of a.o. "The joy of money".

C

Car (company)

Some of us love it although it's simply a vehicle provided by a firm for the business and private use of an employee.

First of all, it is a benefit in kind which can be an integral part of the remuneration and which in many countries remains taxable.

However, the pain of taxation is often mitigated for many (mostly male) employees by the size and glamour of the equipment provided, which they could not afford on their own.

opposite: train, bus, walk
see also: benefit in kind, remuneration

Carbon copy

Originally, carbon copy (cc) was a carbon copy made with carbon paper. Nowadays, carbon copy means the function in e-mail software that allows the user to send a message to any number of addresses.

However, the recipients of the e-mail can see which addresses the e-mail was sent to.

Carbon copies are just as bad at cluttering up the inbox as emails whose content is limited to FYI. Many managers set up an extra inbox for the CC, and read them once a week, if at all.

Remember, where you are in CC, you are not meant to be the addressee and are not expected to respond.

see also: blind carbon copy (BCC), FYI (for your info)

Cash

In corporate finance, the term cash is usually used as an expression.

Cash flow, for example, refers to cash flow. Free cash flow is the free cash flow, i.e. the cash that represents the self-financing capacity of a company obtained during the year and which is not intended to buy new assets nor to pay debts.

The term cash is also used for a payment method. Cash payment means paying for a product or service in cash, nor using credit nor the possibility of payment in instalments.

opposite: no cash, payment in instalments
see also: working capital

Certification

Certifications are granted to show that individuals or organisation have demonstrated and maintain knowledge in a selected technical aspects such as Management (e.g. ISO 9001) or Environment (e.g. ISO 14001) or even CSR (e.g. B-Lab Certification).

Sticking to the principles of the certification obtained by one's organisation allows employees to understand the processes more quickly and to retain a certain know-how since it is documented. Unfortunately, many organisations get certified but do not really follow the principles of their certification.

"Theory is when you know everything and nothing works. Practice is when everything works and nobody knows why. Here we have brought theory and practice together: Nothing works... and nobody knows why!" *Albert Einstein*[8]

see also: QM, QHSE

---

[8] German mathematician and physicist who developed the special and general theories of relativity.

CFO vs. Chief Performance Officer

In large and medium-sized companies, the CFO (Chief Finance Officer) can today rely on digital transformation and data processing and analysis technologies that are gaining momentum within the executive committee, or even position himself as a true business partner thanks to quality data and relevant information in real time. This "connected" CFO and instantaneous translator of the organisation's economic performance is seen by many as the new prince charming of shareholders and some start dreaming of this Chief Performance Officer (CPO) who is praised by many "troubadours".

Digitalisation created the dream of a CPO. The CPO, a child of digitalisation, has inherited the best fruits of his parents' labour: accounting and controlling. As digitalisation takes over much of the manual work of finance departments, CFOs and their teams are increasingly free to do more value-added work and take on a strategic leadership role that was often denied them due to lack of time or resources.

Thus, the CFO, who was in charge of managing data input, finds himself simply organising the input to extract the substantial marrow from the output. Data science is thus entering corporate finance and transforming the CFO into a business partner who, beyond the financial report, will influence the strategy, or even be the real director of its implementation. The Chief Performance Officer has just been born.

For all CFOs and their team, this new paradigm implies the acquisition (or recruitment) of new skills, well beyond "hard skills" with employees capable of processing data or having an end-to-end vision of a process but also "soft skills" to communicate, federate around projects and play the role of an ambassador.

These new pre-requisites for the position could have a positive impact on the attractiveness of the CFO's job, but also on the entire job landscape that could lead to this position. In fact, in addition to the increased interest of the missions within the job itself, these new skills are particularly valuable on the job market, especially in the context of increasingly less linear careers.

opposite: accountant
see also: C-Suite, data analyst, digitalisation

Change Management

Change management is defined as the methods and means by which a company describes and implements change in its internal and external processes.

Changes mostly fail for human reasons: change managers have not taken into account the healthy, real and predictable reactions of normal people whose routines are subject to change.

Change management and transformation are two different undertakings: change is top-down, whereas transformation is bottom-up.

opposite: transformation
see also: transformation, communication

Chart (organisation)

An organisation chart (or *org chart*) is a diagram that shows the internal structure of an organisation. The organisation chart allows you to visualise the hierarchy of units and employees in order to better understand the ranks (levels) and formal relationships within the organisation.

However, the organisation chart does not give any information about the real relationships of employees with each other or even about their circles of influence.

The organisation chart, in any case, says a lot about the culture of the company when it meets three conditions:

  - identify all employees in the organisation;
  - be clear about who reports to whom; and
  - be accessible to everyone at all times.

If your position is at the very bottom of the organisation chart, don't forget: *A cubicle is just a padded cell without a door.*

opposite: "we need no boss, we are all co-workers!"
see also: organisation

Churn rate

The churn rate - also referred to as customer attrition rate, customer turnover rate or cancellation rate - is a key figure from economics that indicates how many customers have been lost in relation to the total number of customers in a certain period under consideration.

The customer churn rate is one of the most important key figures in marketing, customer management and customer relationship management. It shows when and how many customers are lost and gives clues as to why profitability may suffer and growth is prevented. Thus, the churn rate is a good indicator for the growth of a company and can give early indications of potential problems.

In a figurative sense, churn rate is also used for employee attrition.

opposite: retention rate
see also: attrition, retention

Coach (business)

Business coaches are usually experienced entrepreneurs and business owners themselves who decide to use their talents to create and develop a business to help other business owners achieve their goals.

While Google is certainly *king* for giving advice to those who want to start or grow their business, business coaches, on the other hand, are able to provide something far more valuable: personalised and tailored advice.

see also: manager, servant leadership

Code of Conduct

A code of ethics and business conduct sets out the ethical principles that govern the decisions and behaviour of a company or organisation, its management and its employees. It provides general guidance on how employees and management should behave, as well as specific advice on how to deal with issues such as harassment, safety and conflicts of interest.

As ethics and conduct must be exemplary at all times, it does not tolerate snide remarks (not even here).

see also: compliance

Competitiveness

Competitiveness is the ability of an organisation to compete effectively or potentially. It therefore refers to its ability to hold a strong position in a market. The evolution of the company's market share is therefore fundamental to assessing competitiveness.

Competitiveness is classically described in two different ways depending on the origin of the factors of this competitiveness: by price or by cost:

- *Price competitiveness* is generally achieved through a policy of economies of scale or the development of technical progress aimed at achieving productivity gains.
- However, lowering production costs can be achieved without productivity gains (lower labour costs or lower raw material costs), and *cost competitiveness* is the outcome.

opposite: non-competitive
see also: advantage, market share, USP

Compliance

The term compliance can mean different things, depending on which specialist area or context you are in at the time.

For example, there is legal compliance, financial compliance, IT compliance, tax compliance, the company's own codes of conduct or so-called compliance guidelines.

What they all have in common is that they are, on the whole, part of the concept of compliance; however, they only ever refer to sub-areas. Compliance itself is therefore first and foremost a generic term.

A short, possible definition could be as follows:

Compliance = fulfilment of obligations and conformity to rules.

In concrete terms, compliance means adherence to legal provisions and the company's own rules.

Compliance therefore actually refers to a mere matter of course, namely that companies and their employees must also comply with legal regulations. And, of course, to the rules they set for themselves.

see also: code of conduct, non-conformity

Commodity

A commodity is a type of widely available product that is not markedly dissimilar from one unit to another and that is interchangeable with other goods of the same type.

By definition, a commodity product lacks a unique selling point (USP).

opposite: speciality
see also: USP

Communication

„Two monologues do not make a dialogue." Jeff Daly[9]

Communication is the essential tool of management. Whatever management decides, it will have to be communicated, sometimes even repeated over and over again.

Communication can be informative, directive, empathetic, crisis, motivating and at its best inspiring.

opposite: miscommunication
see also: change, management, vision

Contractor

A contractor is a person or company that works on a contractual basis, negotiating agreements with different clients or suppliers to work on specific jobs or projects.

Unlike employees, contractors do not do regular work for a single employer. Instead, they work for a number of different clients as required.

In short, a contractor is a person who has only free time and sells some of it to individuals, groups of people or organisations.

Opposite: employee
See also: freelancer

Controlling

There is no uniform, binding definition of controlling and there probably won't be one in the future either, because academics set different emphases and the practical design in the companies depends strongly on the circumstances in these companies.

Two types of controlling are usually identified:

Financial controlling: it supervises the preparation of the annual financial statements and provides informative data from the reports. This form of controlling is also entrusted with the authenticity of financial reports, compliance with regulations and the analysis of financial data.

---

[9] American designer, specialising in museum gallery and exhibition design.

Project controlling: It ensures that project goals are achieved to the desired quality, while meeting planned deadlines and costs. As a rule, project management is responsible for project controlling.

see also: CFO, finance, project

Cooperation

Cooperation is people or group of people working together to achieve results or people helping each other out to achieve a common goal.

While cooperation between companies always bears the risk of falling into the punitive rules of the market cartel, cooperation between people is praiseworthy.

Cooperation and competition are natural, they occur in every human and animal society; better said, they are both useful and necessary.

The problem is therefore not to have one prevail over the other, but to ensure a good balance between the two. Indeed, one should not be naive and think that cooperation is the ideal to be achieved at the expense of competition. One should not fall into the trap of wanting to impose cooperation as yet another concept after all those that academic managers have tried to plant on the clean slate of what they believe to be an organisation.

A good balance between the two is often what creates good team dynamics.

opposite: competition
see also: manager, team

Corporate social responsibility (CSR)

The ISO 26000 standard defines CSR as: an organisation's responsibility for the impacts of its decisions and activities on society and the environment, through transparent and ethical behavior that:

- contributes to Sustainable Development, including health and the welfare of society;
- takes into account the expectations of stakeholders;
- is in compliance with applicable law and consistent with international norms of behaviour;
- and is integrated throughout the organisation and implemented in its relations.

Beware! CSR is not just a series of cosmetic measures to reduce its environmental impact or improve its social impact. When CSR is implemented correctly, based on good CSR practices, it has the potential to improve the overall functioning of the company, to make it more efficient, more resilient, more agile. For all these reasons, CSR is generally considered to be a factor of productivity gains and financial performance for companies.

„Without restoring an ethos of social responsibility, there can be no meaningful and sustained economic recovery." *Jeffrey Sachs*[10]

see also: compliance, environment, ethic

Creditor

A creditor is an organisation or person who people owe money to. Therefore, your suppliers are your creditors.

If you have a question about the payment to a supplier, you'll ask the creditor accountant (also called account payables accountant) of your organisation, or you gently wait for the angry call of the supplier.

opposite: debitor
see also: accountant, finance, supplier

Crisis

"There cannot be a crisis next week. My schedule is already full." *Henry Kissinger*[11]

A crisis is a determined or undetermined event that affects the regular business activities in such a way that people and society can come to harm and material assets are destroyed in the process.

A crisis becomes a serious crisis when there is an issue in external communication or when the person(s) causing the crisis behaves in such a way that the audience can build up an enemy image.

As most crises originate from decisions that should have been taken a long time ago, it is important for a manager not to let problems linger and dream that they will be solved over time.

see also: communication, risk, risk management

---

[10] American economist, academic, public policy analyst and former director of The Earth Institute at Columbia University.

[11] American politician, diplomat, and geopolitical consultant who served as United States Secretary of State and National Security Advisor under the presidential administrations of Richard Nixon and Gerald Ford.

C-Suite

A popular term in companies which have on the same floor the offices of Chief executive officer, Chief financial officer, Chief operation officer and possibly other Chiefs as well.

This level of management is also called CxO as the "x" can be interchanged with the letter designating the person's function as we wish (e.g. CPO for Chief Purchasing Officer or sometimes Chief Performance Officer or sometimes Chief Production Officer... perhaps not the best example!)

opposite: cubicle
see also: manager, board (of directors)

Customer

They always want something more and pay less, they ask for it today but wanted it yesterday, and above all, as in Verdi's Rigoletto, they are as fickle as a feather in the wind: that is the definition of customers.

More commonly, the customer is a person, a group of people or an organisation that receives or can receive goods, services, products or ideas from another person in exchange for payment.

Since the customers are the sole source of your turnover, it is essential to put them at the centre of your concerns.

opposite: no customer
see also: turnover, vision

Data analyst

Data analysts are responsible for the analysis of data from the company's activities. They collect and process the data in order to submit relevant recommendations. The aim of their tasks is to bring the data to life by interpreting it.

In other words, they use statistical techniques and IT tools to support and facilitate decision-making through the analysis of quantitative and qualitative data.

"If the statistics are boring, then you've got the wrong numbers." *Edward Tufte*[12]

opposite: superstitious controller
see also: business plan, strategy

Days payable outstanding (DPO)

Days Payable Outstanding (DPO) refers to the average number of days it takes a company to pay back its accounts payable. Therefore, the

---

[12] Also called „ET". American statistician and professor emeritus of political science, statistics, and computer science at Yale University.

DPO shows how well an organisation is managing its accounts payable by measuring the average number of days it takes you to pay vendors.

DPO = accounts payable x number of days / Cost of Goods Sold (COGS).

Here, COGS refers to beginning inventory plus purchases subtracting the ending inventory.

opposite: days sales outstanding
see also: cash, working capital

Days sales outstanding (DSO)

Days sales outstanding (DSO) is the average number of days that receivables remain outstanding before they are collected. It is used to determine the effectiveness of a company's credit and collection efforts in allowing credit to customers, as well as its ability to collect from them.

DSO = (accounts receivable ÷ revenue) × number of days

Here, the revenue and the number of days are to be considered over the same period of time (monthly, quarterly or annually).

opposite: days payable outstanding
see also: cash, working capital

Deadlines

"I love deadlines. I like the whooshing sound they make as they fly by." *Douglas Adams*

The deadline has nothing to do with the death that awaits you beyond that line. However, psychologically the word deadline will be harder to hear than the expression delivery date.

Think about this when you are talking to someone who is sensitive.

see also: delivery date

Deduction

A deduction is an expense that can be subtracted from a taxpayer's gross income to reduce the amount of income subject to tax.

Let us be clear: this is a tax term and only a tax term. In other *languages* we speak of expenditure, investment, acquisition of assets, etc.

opposite: surcharge
see also: accountant, asset, tax

Delivery date

Psychologically softer than the word deadline, the expression delivery date means the same thing when taken out of its logistical context, it refers to work expected by a client, a boss or a colleague.

The delivery date should always be mentioned to employees who are given a job by the manager, otherwise the deadline may turn into a patience game.

opposite: open
see also: deadline, supply chain

Delocalisation

Delocalisation refers to the transfer of activities, capital and jobs from one company to another in order to benefit from competitive advantages, i.e. more favourable economic conditions:

- low wages,
- more flexible labour laws,
- weak currency,
- lower taxes,
- economic dynamism,
- existence of a technological pole,
- environment,
- etc.

Relocation has, moreover, been favoured by the fall in transport costs and the globalisation of capital and markets, which have led to a fall in customs tariffs.

This migration takes place mainly from the country of origin to abroad, but it can also be from an urban area to a rural area or vice versa, for the same reasons.

Strictly speaking, relocation concerns all activities and amounts to separating the places of production from those of consumption. But given the vertical division of labour at global level, delocalisation often takes place by segment of the activity process.

opposite: repatriation
see also: advantage

Depreciation

Stop thinking that depreciation is the same as amortisation because it is not!

Depreciation is only for tangible assets (items having value, AND that you can touch) while amortisation is for intangible assets (items having value, BUT that you can't touch).

As you may have noticed, I have simply reversed the definition of amortisation.

opposite: amortisation
see also: amortisation, asset

Differentiation

What makes you or your product so different from other products on the market?

Differentiation refers to the results of efforts to make a brand stand out to customers. Specifically, it distinguishes itself as a provider of unique value. Differentiation can come from the technology used, from the particular service provided to the customer, from being part of a particular circle, or even from all of these sources.

Let's take the example of Dyson and its vacuum cleaners: a new technology, with a particular design and a service in the shop where you buy it (a floor mat in front of the products) and the impression given to the customers that they belong to a particular circle. In the end, they will only have bought a vacuum cleaner!

opposite: integration
see also: advantage, customer

Digitalisation

Digitisation is the use of digital technologies to change a business model and provide new revenue and value generation opportunities; it is the process of moving to a digital business.

However, the term digitalisation is often variable in different companies and environments. A segmentation of digitalisation within an organisation is common.

In practice, it must be understood that the digitalisation of a company is a part of the strategy; like any strategy, it must also and above all be for the benefit of the customer to be successful. This is why most digitalisation initiatives are driven by customer demand.

opposite: analog (if any)
see also: change management, customer, transformation

Director

The term director comes from Latin and means "one who leads". In everyday language it will be used for many positions in the organisation, sometimes even positions that do not have the name *director*.

However, four types of directors appear most often in business language:

- *non-executive directors*: not involved in the daily running of the firm. They are tasked with bringing an independent third-party perspective in the decision-making process.
- *executive director*: involved in the daily running of the organisation. They are involved in making decisions that affect daily operations.
- *managing directors*: appointed by the rest of the directors and are solely responsible for daily company operations. They are typically known as Chief Executive Officer and are executive director.
- *de facto or shadow directors*: they do not have an official title. However, they have some influence on the decisions of the board of directors. Never underestimate their power in the organisation.

The de facto and shadow directors obtain this title because they can do it.

"The question, *who should be boss?* is like asking, *who should be the tenor of the quartet?* Obviously, the man who can sing tenor." *Henry Ford*

see also: leader, manager

Disruptive innovation

While innovation in general often refers to an improvement of a process, a product, a solution etc. that seems innovative, disruptive innovation does not aim to improve the process but to make it completely obsolete. Thus, we are no longer talking about added value but about the creation of new value.

Clayton Christensen[13] first explained the concept in 1995 and identified a process for achieving disruptive innovation:

---

[13] American academic and business consultant who developed the theory of "disruptive innovation", which has been called the most influential business idea of the early 21st century.

- First, a new product or service with new features appears. This product/service is not necessarily better than others on the market, but it has differentiating characteristics.
- A niche of users dissatisfied with existing solutions is attracted to this new product.
- This product is constantly being improved and is gaining more and more market share.
- Other market players ignore these new features and remain focused on the most profitable part of the market.
- The new market is becoming more and more important and the other players are faced with a dilemma: adapt and risk destroying a business model that has been profitable until now or do nothing and risk being pushed out by the other players.

But be careful! Nowadays the word disruption is misused for everything. It is trendy.

opposite: innovation
see also: innovation, market share

Diversification

Diversification is a strategic version of risk management. It involves integrating a range of investments that form part of a portfolio to minimise risk or volatility, by investing in a wide variety of instruments, asset classes, sectors or markets.

The idea is that a portfolio composed of various investments will, on average, produce higher returns and have lower risk than any single investment within that particular portfolio.

The term diversification applies not only to the stock market portfolio but also to the different sectors of activity of companies.

opposite: all-eggs-in-one-basket
see also: risk management, strategy

Diversity

A successful organisation in which individuals of different race, ethnicity, religious belief, socio-economic status, language, geographic origin, gender and/or sexual orientation contribute their different knowledge, backgrounds, experiences and interests to the benefit of their diverse business community is the definition of diversity and it applies unreservedly to any business.

The success of the diverse organisation depends on everyone contributing to the success of the organisation by embracing difference and making it a driving force. Individuals in a healthy, diverse organisation practice daily understanding and respect for the different ideas, opinions and unique perspectives of those who are somewhat different from them, recognising that these individuals share and actively work towards many common goals for the benefit of the organisation as a whole.

opposite: do you really need it?
see also: organisation, success

Dropping (name)

Name-dropping is often criticised and has a negative connotation when it is mentioned.

Done intelligently, name-dropping can open doors in your job search. After all, it is a way of instantly having something in common with someone you have never met. It's like a de facto reference that you can use to establish your credibility long before you get to that stage.

However, be on your guard: only do this after you have obtained (even tacit) agreement from the person mentioned, don't add to it to make yourself look good, don't drop the name of someone you don't know and definitely don't pull out a catalogue of names in a conversation... unless you're applying for a job as a phone book.

opposite: „I have no acquaintance"
see also: business card

E

EBIT

Earnings Before Interest and Tax. It is an indicator of the company's profitability and is found in the *Profit and Loss* (P&L) section.

EBIT is often referred to as operating income since they both exclude taxes and interest expenses in their calculations.

see also: EBITDA, EBT, purpose

EBITDA

Earnings before interest, taxes, depreciation and amortisation is another widely used indicator to measure a company's financial performance and project its earnings potential.

EBITDA ignores debt financing and depreciation and amortisation costs in the calculation of profitability. It also excludes taxes and interest costs on debt. EBITDA therefore enables an in-depth analysis of the profitability of a company's operating performance.

EBITDA is an important measure in private equity as it is also used to indicate the level of debt of a private company. The "B" and "I" in

EBITDA stand for "Before Interest", i.e. the cash needed to service the debt comes from EBITDA.

In simple words, if EBITDA is too low or negative, the company cannot repay its loans. To assess a private company's level of debt and its ability to service its debt, acquiring organisations use debt ratios as an indicator of the health or risk of the company.

see also: debt ratio, EBIT, private equity, merger, acquisition

EBT

Earnings Before Tax.
The pain only follows!

see also: dividends, EBIT, EBITDA, tax

Education

Usually defined as the process of imparting or acquiring particular knowledge or skills, as for a profession, it has nothing to do with intelligence. Several studies have apparently proven that there is a correlation between education and intelligence, and in particular that education might increase intelligence within the framework of abstract thinking.

Nevertheless, Elon Musk brought it to the point: "I hate when people confuse education with intelligence, you can have a bachelor's degree and still be an idiot." I wonder if he also thought of including other degree holders.

opposite: intelligence (sometimes)
see also: job description

Elephant

It's the biggest animal in the room and nobody says, "There's an elephant in the room."

The main problem in many organisations is that the meeting participants do not dare to address the issues when the manager is present. It is the role of the manager to create an environment of trust so that he or she can also see that there is an elephant in the room.

opposite: mouse?
see also: speak up, trust

Enterprise resource planning (ERP)

An ERP is a management software that integrates numerous functionalities allowing to manage all the services of the company such as: stock management, production management, CRM (Customer Relationship Management), Accounting, Quality... It centralises all the operational flows of the company as well as all the data on a unique basis.

From a structural point of view, the ERP software is the backbone of the company. It is a central tool in the company's information system. It is common to all employees and is at the heart of everyone's tasks and objectives. Employees have access to the data they are interested in and thus become more autonomous and productive.

For the general management and the various department managers, this tool will also facilitate the management of the activity thanks to advanced reporting and Business Intelligence functionalities.

opposite: abacus, pencil
see also: controlling, intelligence

Environment

Environment is the term that encompasses everything that surrounds the organisation. From humans (social) to animals and plants (ecological), water and air (elemental) to the market in which it operates (economic).

Increasingly concerned about the environment and the well-being of their employees, a large number of organisations have decided to become more involved in the environmental cause.

Obviously, not all companies have the same degree of involvement. Some will simply choose to integrate sustainable development values into their strategy, while others will opt for the implementation of environmental management or have an approach based on corporate social responsibility.

More and more organisations are adopting a sustainable development approach for a number of reasons.

First, it allows them to reduce their costs, and secondly, it improves their brand image because people are increasingly sensitive to sustainable development. Thanks to this, they can differentiate themselves from the competition but also innovate.

Second, the fact that a company integrates sustainable development into the heart of its management strategy has positive repercussions on the well-being of its employees. Indeed, it forces them to take social issues into account. Employees are therefore more motivated and consequently more involved in the organisation's activities.

But be careful not to fall into greenwashing!

opposite: non-eco-friendly
see also: differentiation, greenwashing, innovation

Ethic

Business ethics is the application of ethical principles or values to the conduct of business; it concerns all discretionary and unregulated decisions and behaviour.

The main difference between *ethics* and *ethos* is that ethics refers to a set of moral principles whereas ethos refers to character or customs or a set of attitudes and values. Ethics is derived from the word ethos, however, in today's world, these two words are used separately.

opposite: immorality
see also: compliance

Equality (gender)

Originally, gender equality ensures that every person, man or woman, can participate actively and fruitfully in the development of his or her life, community and society, without being discriminated against solely on the basis of being a man or a woman.

Today, gender equality must be considered beyond the biological differentiation of the term and take into account the social gender of the person. This change of parameter does not take place in all countries and sometimes within a country, regional legislations can be different. Similarly, some regional cultures may also reject the concept.

The aim here is not to impose the vision of gender equality in the social sense, but rather to see the emergence of a humanist manager who understands this notion. The humanist manager will have to go beyond the legislative rules and embrace the differences in order to make none.

Recently, the concept of gender equality has been broadened to discard the traditional idea that there are only two genders: women and men (gender binarity). It includes people of all genders and recognises that people whose gender identity and expression is non-binary often experience the same kind of inequality as women.

"You are not born a woman, you become one" *Simone de Beauvoir*[14]

opposite: inequality of rights
see also: diversity, gender, humanism

Equity

The equity of a company includes the share capital and other equity. It corresponds to the sums paid by the partners or shareholders, increased by the profits generated annually by the company which are not distributed as dividends.

This financial concept of the company equity is to be distinguished from the term equity in its legal meaning. The aim of (legal) equity is to ensure that everyone is treated fairly, equally and reasonably. This principle is used when the strict application of (legal) rules would lead to unfair consequences for one of the parties.

see also: financial statement

Exit interview

The exit interview is a meeting between at least one representative of the company's human resources department and the departing employee. In this particular interview, the employee has most often resigned, but it may very well be a retirement, the end of a contract.

The exit interview is an opportunity to actively contribute to improving the working environment in the company and to leave a good impression (for both parties). It may be too late for the departing employee, but his or her contribution can make a positive difference to the situation of the staying colleagues.

Conducting an exit interview is an integral part of a good hire to retire process.

opposite: onboarding
see also: hire to retire, onboarding

Expense

Stop thinking that expense is the same as expenditure because it's not!

---

[14] French writer, intellectual, existentialist philosopher, political activist, feminist, and social theorist. Her contributions to the fields of ethics, politics, existentialism, phenomenology and feminist theory and her significance as an activist and public intellectual is a matter of record.

An expense is a cost that has been incurred by an organisation or company to earn revenues during a specific period.

Expenditure refers to the amount incurred by a company or an organisation after purchasing an asset or reduction of liability among others.

In accounting, an expenditure is recorded at a single point in time (the time of purchase), compared to an expense that is recorded in a period where it has been used up or expired.

opposite: income
see also: accounting, investment

Export

From a customs point of view, export is a departure of goods from the domestic territory.

Generally, export is also used to refer to goods but also services delivered outside the domestic territory.

In order to avoid misunderstandings, limit yourself to speaking of export in the case of delivery of goods to another country.

opposite: import
see also: logistic, supply chain

F

Facsimile (fax)

For those over fifty, it is a painful memory of youth. Facsimile (also called fax or telefax by the initiated) is the transmission by telephone of a scanned printed document to a telephone number connected to a printer or other receiving device. Both the sender and receiver are fax machines.

In the not so ancient days, when human beings communicated mainly by letter and telephone, facsimile made it possible to transmit printed matter without using the postal service. The transmission was instantaneous as long as the recipient did not forget to put paper in the receiving printer.

There is no reason to know this term nowadays but, as some organisations are still using fax, it deserves its place in this glossary.

opposite: who cares nowadays?
see also: communication

Fatigue (change)

Continuous improvement is a business necessity but also and certainly a human need. The problem is that most organisations are simply not organised for continuous change. Continuous change does not mean bombarding your employees with one change after another. This approach has led to a growing and costly problem – "change fatigue".

Change fatigue is associated with increased stress, burnout and especially reduced organisational commitment. It is somewhat akin to passive resignation. It is this passive resignation that can make change fatigue more problematic than the "resistance to change" that most leaders talk about and that is measured over time along the Kübler-Ross curve.

They are 5 steps that can limit or help to avoid change fatigue

1. Define a clear target to be reach and share it as "the vision"
2. Approach the change as a cross-functional project in identifying all stakeholders' skills impacted
3. The change in the organisation relies on the skills of the leaders
4. Enable high levels of employee engagement
5. Establish an action plan following a timeline adapted to the capability of your team

Following these five steps can help reduce and prevent change fatigue in your organisation. At any time, they need to be supported by a clear communication around the change and the achievements (small or big). The management is leading the change, the employees make the change, and only then, the organisation changes.

opposite: relaxing environment
see also: change, Kübler-Ross curve, transformation

Feasibility study

The feasibility study assesses the viability of an idea, project, technology or new business. The objective is to identify all relevant aspects related to the development of the intention and to determine whether, after taking into account all relevant factors, the business intention is commercially attractive.

There are generally three types of feasibility studies:

- *Technical feasibility*: to determine the technological feasibility of the idea or innovation;
- *Market feasibility*: to understand the commercial value of the idea or market in which your business will operate; and
- *Commercial feasibility*: after determining that there is a market for the idea or innovation, to determine the financial requirements to make it viable.

At the end of the feasibility study, the organisation should have a clear understanding of the business opportunity of the idea or innovation and the strategy to make it a successful venture. It will also highlight the resources needed to implement it and the risks involved.

If you think that once the study is completed and the result accepted by your peers, it will open all the doors to the desired investment with the management of your organisation, you are just wrong. It may take weeks, months, years or even never happen.

opposite: blind flight
see also: direction, innovation, hope

Financial statement

A financial statement is a financial report that is prepared annually for an organisation. In other words, it is a report on the (financial) situation or achievements of the organisation during a year.

The annual financial report always includes the balance sheet and profit and loss account, the accounting records, their audit (if any), their confirmation and, if necessary, their publication. In addition, it can and should also be supplemented in part by a management report, in which the company's current situation, opportunities and risks are presented. The latest depends on the size of the organisation.

opposite: unreported business
see also: EBIT, EBITDA, EBIT, Profit (and Loss)

Fixed asset

It is a long-term tangible asset. The term fixed refers to the fact that those assets can usually not be converted into cash easily, such as land or buildings.

opposite: current asset
see also: asset, amortisation

Free

Free does not exist! If something is free, it means that someone has already paid for it before or that you will pay for it later.

In the social media business, when an app is free, the product is not the app but the user. The user is sold to advertisers in the best cases; in the worst cases, the user's personal data is sold and used for sometimes murky purposes.

Even tax free does not really exist!

opposite: priced
see also: advantage, differentiation, price, tax

Freelancer

Freelance means working as a self-employed person. The status of a self-employed person is that of a natural person who is an entrepreneur, owner and employee at the same time.

Many sources prove that the word was not first used by Sir Walter Scott[15] in 1819 in his famous book Ivanhoe, but the original meaning is no less false: The term is simple and self-explanatory. A mercenary soldier offers his labour and weapons (his lance) to the highest bidder. He is a freelancer!

Philosophically, the freelancer is not so different from the employee; if we assume that both have only free time available and that both sell some of it to an employer.

opposite: employee (not philosophical!)

Free zone

A free zone is a geographical area of a territory that offers tax advantages. For example, VAT exemptions, income tax exemptions or exemptions from customs duties (import or export taxes). The aim is to attract investors and develop economic activity in an area deemed a priority by the authorities. Internationally, free zones are often located in major ports or near borders.

In 2018, the OECD identified more than 3,500 free zones in 130 countries or economies in North and South America, the Asia-Pacific

---

[15] The first use can be found in *The Life and Times of Hugh Miller* by Thomas N. Brown published in 1809. However, I prefer to attribute the first use to Ivanhoe, the hero of my childhood.

region, Europe and Africa, up from 79 in 25 countries or economies in 1975.[16]

opposite: wherever you tax business at a regular tax rate
see also: advantage, competition, export, tax

Fund

A fund is a special-purpose vehicle funded by several investors. The money paid in is called the fund's assets. This money is invested by the fund manager in shares, bonds, precious metals, commodities or other types of investments depending on the type of fund.

opposite: saving account
see also: managed funds

Fusion

A fusion is a merger of two companies of different sizes.

However, the term *merger* has broadened over the last two decades and now often includes the merger of two commercial enterprises of different sizes. In the past, merger was only used for companies of the same size.

If the two merging companies are competitors, the merger is said to be a horizontal integration, if a supplier and a customer merge, it is said to be vertical.

opposite: demerger, spin-off
see also: acquisition, horizontal integration, merger, vertical integration

Fusion marketing

Merger marketing defines the cooperation between two companies that are not competitors but have a common target audience and values, aiming to achieve strategic goals with a reduced investment. This cooperation involves the development of a common and profitable strategy to attract new customers.

This approach, which is frequently used in marketing, is often compared to guerrilla warfare, where like-minded groups join forces to fight. Betrayal might lurk in the shadows, around the corner.

---

[16] OECD.org: *Free trade zones are being used to traffic counterfeit goods*, 2018.

opposite: marketing
see also: advantage, cooperation

FYI (For your Info)

FYI (for your information) are the three letters that best pollute the manager's email box. If the sender's intention is neutral, with the idea of keeping the boss or colleagues informed on the progress of a subject, these three letters, FYI, most often denote a stereotypical attitude.

FYI can actually have three meanings:

- from now on, you cannot say that I have not kept you informed;
- if you could react then I would not be obliged to take a stand and therefore take responsibility; and
- I'm going to decide something stupid but you didn't stop me even though you knew.

It is important for managers to educate their staff not to use these three letters, which waste time and discredit staff by sending time-consuming and unnecessary emails. I just advise this FYI.

opposite: as requested
see also: BC (blind copy), CC (carbon copy)

G

Game changer

Behind the almost mythical definition of game changers as those who go beyond the traditional boundaries of business and achieve great success, the game changer is a person or organisation that through a disruptive approach to a market or a product has been able to change the rules of an established market or exponentially increase an unformulated market demand.

It is a question of disrupting the market either by a new idea and an appropriate approach or by means of targeted research. The most recent examples are Dyson and his vacuum cleaner, Apple and the iPhone or even the computer mouse; but long before the technological age as we know it, we can mention Henry Ford with the Model T, or Christopher Columbus and his new India route. The latter being a real *random* game changer, as he opened the way to a new continent and never set foot in India.

But let's not forget that the game changer is also an exceptional communicator. Without appropriate communication, the game changer does not exist because the disruptive approach or product would remain under the radar and therefore unsuccessful.

opposite: mainstream
see also: advantage, communication, disruption

Gender

Most cultures use the binary approach to gender, with two genders; those who exist outside these groups are usually referred to by the generic term non-binary. But gender cannot be reduced to an anatomical issue.

Many communities, and meanwhile even countries, defend and claim that there are many different social gender identities, including male, female, transgender, gender-neutral, non-binary, agender, pangender, genderqueer, two-spirit, third gender, and all, none, or a combination of these.

One could apparently identify between 50 and 70 different genders, depending on the approaches taken. It is not possible to list them all here without certainly making serious errors of definition.

One thing is certain: managers have to embrace the difference in social genders as they deal with collaborators, employees, teams. The gender of the employee (or manager), no matter which one a particular person chooses, does not change what an organisation requires from the manager nor from the employee.

opposite: the opposite of gender is surely a gender as well
see also: diversity

Give-away

"Small gifts maintain friendship. The first person who said this wanted to be offered something." *Eugène Scribe*[17]

Little things that are worthless but show a certain attachment to the relationship between two people or between two organisations. These are the giveaways.

Gone are the days of invitations to hunting trips, yachts or exotic and luxurious places. Compliance rules ensuring the independence of economic actors and, above all, their exemplary behaviour have meant that all these lavish ways no longer exist. And that is a good thing.

However, the give-away has remained in fashion, so much so that some legislators have codified it and defined it by a legally acceptable maximum value.

---

[17] French dramatist and opera librettist.

After a few years as a manager, you will find most of these gifts in your children's toy box or in the kitchen drawers, the floor of your car or in the cellar; pens, boxes with obscure uses, bottle openers and other small things that are no longer useful. You will appreciate them all the same: the business card will soon no longer exist, so we needed to exchange something, didn't we?

opposite: nothing
see also: benefit in kind, compliance, value

Goal

Stop thinking that a goal is similar to an objective, because it is not!

While a goal is a general guideline that explains what the organisation wants to achieve, the objective defines the strategy or implementation steps needed to reach the goal.

Thus, a goal without implementation plan is called a wish.

opposite: carpe diem
see also: action plan, KPI, objective

Governance

Governance is a word that hardly has an equivalent outside English-speaking countries. Governance is defined by ISO 26000 as the system by which an organisation makes and implements decisions in pursuit of its objectives.

Today, the term corporate governance encompasses the entire management and control processes of a company. It concerns the internal order, including regulations and directives, the control functions and their means.

While the term originally described only the procedures of shareholder control over the management of a company, governance has been broadened so that, for example, the relationships between the various stakeholders, the internal structures of company management or external factors are also better taken into account.

opposite: mismanagement
see also: controlling, management, stakeholder

Greenwashing

Greenwashing (or green sheen) describes the practice of misusing green positioning or practices for marketing purposes. Greenwashing can for example be done through misleading advertisements or by displaying unofficial "home-made green labels".

The line between greenwashing and legitimate argumentation or laudable corporate practice is sometimes blurred and subjective. Therefore it is difficult to defend against the accusation of greenwashing when the practice was not intended. One of the growing examples is the production of electricity in nuclear power plants: its promoters point to the absence of CO_2 emissions; its detractors speak of greenwashing and point to the hundreds of years of radiation caused by nuclear waste.

Beyond the ethical problem raised by the practice, greenwashing is likely to be considered as misleading advertising; in this case, it is a criminal offence and is neither emotional nor subjective!

opposite: ecological, sustainable
see also: CSR, Environment, sustainability

H

Hedge funds

„I don't think that hedge funds are bad per se. I think they're just one more financial tool. And in that sense, they're useful." *Barack Obama*

To understand what a hedge fund is, you need to know what an investment fund and a hedge are. If the latter is understood by its name, the word hedge determines the former.

A hedge is a transaction that aims to reduce exposure to risk. A hedge transaction may, for example, consist of buying an asset whose value moves in the opposite direction to a second asset acquired at the same time.

The hedge fund is managed by a fund manager, who usually owns a significant portion of the fund, which speculates on market movements using three main tools:

- *Short selling*: this involves selling an asset that you do not own, with the aim of buying it back later at a lower price in order to return it to the owner who lent the security. It has a cost, as the lender has to be paid and liquidity constraints are important.

- *Arbitrage*: these are financial products whose price is derived from the price of an asset called the "underlying asset". The aim is to exploit unjustified price differences.
- *Leverage*: the aim is to increase exposure to a security. It is measured in ratio, which is the ratio between the assets under control and the amount invested. It provides additional liquidity and multiplies gains.

opposite: mutual funds
see also: acquisition, asset

Hire to Retire

Hire to Retire is a holistic HR process organised around a fictitious employee who would ideally spend his or her entire career in one and only one company. The main stages of this fictional career are:

- *Planning*: planning the position and its content
- *Recruiting*: this includes choosing external recruiters, employer branding, advertisements, participation in job fairs, etc.
- *Payroll*: including all legal obligations related to employment (including social security, taxes, benefits in kind, etc.)
- *Employee management*: The salary is only one part of the relationship with the employee. Employee management includes ongoing training, performance evaluation and planning for possible advancement.
- *Relocation*: e.g., expatriation abroad.
- *Retirement*: leaving the company including exit interview, company pension, etc.

opposite: no HR management
see also: human resource, talent management, exit interview

Hope

Hope has nothing to do with business, but they are intimately linked. Business is about hard work, tenacity, resilience, sometimes patience, but also passion; just as hope is the last thing to die.

When an employee or worse, a manager says they have hope for the success of a project, then call HR and work on replacing that person. Business is not based on hope even though you will often encounter hope mongers on your way through the business jungle.

opposite: hopeless
see also: business plan, vision

Horizontal integration

Horizontal integration refers to the acquisition of a related company or another company that operates at the same level of the value chain in a defined industry.

opposite: vertical integration
see also: merger & acquisition, value chain

Humanistic management

The success of companies is no longer measured only in terms of profit but also by the impact on their social and natural environment. More and more ethical funds require a certain transparency. The humanistic dimension of a company defines its qualification even more than the ISO standard in certain sectors.

Humanism is today the essential factor in the success of companies:

–   *The humanist company vs. empathetic management:* the humanist company is an organisation committed to respecting the well-being of its employees and the environment. Although for a long time the notion of employee well-being has focused on material and working conditions, the humanist company is concerned not to forget the relational conditions, particularly the direct hierarchical relationship, but also the values promoted and lived within the organisation and towards the stakeholders in the economic action. This so-called humanist positioning is not opposed to the intrinsic goal of the company, which is to generate profits. Empathy applies essentially to the character of the manager (and not to an organisation), which will mark its organisation by its psychometric profile more than by a transformation of the organisation's relationship with its environment. Thus, the humanist company sets the organisation in a sustainable culture to which employees at all hierarchical levels are invited to adhere, whereas the empathetic manager will only influence by his behaviour his four dimensions and his environment.
–   *Humanism and trust:* Let's be frank: the purpose of humanism in the company is not productivity. If the idea is to make more

profit, employees will not be tricked, they will consider the approach as manipulation and will not adhere to the project. On the other hand, if the aim is truly material and relational well-being with the stakeholders, productivity can result, as well as commitment and mobilisation.

While empathy is a personal attitude towards others, humanism is a philosophy of conduct applicable to an entire organisation. While empathy can be used as a channel of communication in certain situations, humanism results in coded behaviour that allows the organisation to be transparent, caring and authentic. Humanism is the mother of ethics and the bearer of values essential to the modern organisation.

opposite: empathetic management
see also: trust, servant leadership

Human Capital

Human capital is a measure of the skills, education, capabilities and attributes of the workforce that influence its productive capacity and earning potential. Thus, according to the OECD[18], human capital is defined as the knowledge, skills, competencies and other attributes embodied by individuals or groups of individuals, acquired over a lifetime and used to produce goods, services or ideas under market conditions.

Human capital should not be confused with human resources; while the former develops the knowledge and skills of employees, the latter contributes to improving the quality of life of employees in the organisation.

opposite: incompetency
see also: human resources

Human resources

Human resources is used to describe both the people who work for a company or organisation and the department responsible for managing all matters relating to employees, who collectively represent one of the most valuable resources of any company or organisation (resources).

Human resources should not be confused with human capital.

---

[18] Wesphalen, p. 10.

opposite: one (man- or) woman-show company
see also: human capital

Humour

„The number one premise of business is that it needs not be boring or dull. It ought to be fun. If it's not fun, you're wasting your life." - *Tom Peters*[19]

No further comment.

---

[19] American writer on business management practices, best known for *In Search of Excellence* (co-authored with Robert H. Waterman Jr)

Income statement

It is one of the main financial statements of a company. It shows whether a company is making a profit or a loss for a given period. The income statement, together with the balance sheet and cash flow statement, helps you understand the financial health of your business.

The main items presented in the income statement are:

- *Revenues,* which are the amounts obtained from the sale of goods and/or the rendering of services.
- *Expenses,* which include the cost of goods sold, selling, general and administrative expenses, and interest expense.
- *Profits and losses,* such as the sale of a non-current asset for an amount different from its book value.
- *Net income,* which is the result of subtracting the company's expenses and losses from the company's income and gains.

Incompetence (and not incompetency)

„If you want to do business with us, you are not allowed to make fair comment on our incompetency." *Unknown*

There is a clear difference between incompetence and incompetency: incompetency is the condition of not having the capacity to make the decision while incompetence is the inability to perform.

The word incompetence defines not having the necessary knowledge and therefore being unable to perform. While the term applies primarily to selected people in the organisation, the proliferation of incompetents can result in the organisation becoming incompetent itself. This leads to difficulties with customers and most of the time to the term defined under *Insolvency*.

opposite: competency
see also: PHB – pointed-hair boss

Innovation

Simply put, innovation is the identification and observation of a problem, and then solving it; it is a process by which knowledge creates additional value for the company in the form of a good, service or process.

The challenges of innovation for the company are both:

- Economic: innovation creates and consolidates competitive advantage.
- Societal: innovation serves the company's social responsibility (CSR).

Innovation is an instrument at the service of the strategy by preserving and consolidating the competitive advantage whatever the strategic option of the company.

Any organisation that does not focus on innovation is doomed to disappear. The humanist manager must create an environment that is favourable to innovation. Not to do so is a serious failure.

opposite: banality
see also: patent, unicorn

Inorganic growth

Inorganic growth is about combining one company with another through a merger or acquisition. This provides an immediate increase in assets, revenues and market presence.

The other side of the coin is that it leads to a considerable expansion of management capabilities. There are suddenly many more employees and more assets to monitor, use and dispose of as your business needs change. In addition, growth may take place in unexpected directions.

opposite: organic growth
see also: acquisition, organic growth, PMI

Inspiration

Inspiration is the motivation of the intellect. However, inspiration differs from motivation in that it is endogenous (it comes from within the subject) whereas motivation is exogenous (generated by an intervention outside the subject: money, gift, suffering).

In business as in life in general, if you lack inspiration, take a deep breath.

opposite: motivation
see also: humour, team

Insolvency

Let's make it easy: if you have more debts than assets, you are insolvent.

But keep in mind that it's not because you are insolvent that you are bankrupt while if you are bankrupt, you definitely are insolvent.

opposite: creditworthy
see also: bankruptcy

Intangible asset

To make it simple: if you can't touch it, it has a financial value and you acquired it from someone else, then it is an intangible asset. The most common examples of intangible assets are patents, copyrights, franchises, goodwill, trademarks and trade names.

„The music industry is a strange combination of having real and intangible assets: pop bands are brand names in themselves, and at a given stage in their careers their name alone can practically gaurantee hit records." *Richard Branson*

Intellectual property

The term intellectual property covers a wide range of products: from a particular manufacturing process, to plans for launching a product, to a trade secret such as a chemical formula (e.g. the recipe for a sweetened soft drink) or a list of countries in which your patents are registered.

Intellectual property is the lifeblood of any enduring organisation; innovation turns early ideas into intangible assets, which in turn become the intellectual property of the organisation.

In other words, intellectual property is a category of property that includes the intangible creations of the human intellect.

opposite: tangible assets, brainless organisation (?)
see also: innovation, intangible assets

Intelligence

Whether someone is intelligent or not can be measured but calling someone intelligent or not is usually a subjective and emotional expression of your opinion.

On the other hand, the word intelligence will be used in business to refer to the product resulting from the collection, processing, integration, analysis, evaluation and interpretation of available information. Software for the analysis of financial and operational data will be commonly referred to as Business Intelligence.

opposite: stupidity
see also: controlling, data analyst

Interest

In his epic poem *Inferno*, Alighieri Dante[20] met the usurers - interest collectors - at the bottom of the seventh circle of hell. The torment reserved for them was to sit under a rain of fire, wearing a purse marked with a distinctive sign around their necks. Unfortunately, or fortunately, times have changed!

---

[20] Italian poet, writer and philosopher who lived in Florence (Italy) during the 13th century.

Today, interest is the sum that a borrower pays on top of the capital borrowed when repaying what he owes the lender.

We have learned since 2017 that interest can be both positive and negative. In doing so, savings can also cost interest to those who engage in them and therefore do not invest. This reminds, somehow, of the fourth circle of Dante's hell, where the greedy and the prodigal met.

opposite: depending on the situation, negative or positive interest
see also: debt

Internal rate of return (IRR)

The internal rate of return (IRR) is an important indicator for measuring the relevance of a project. Its principle is simple: it takes into account all the flows (purchases, sales, income, expenses, taxation, etc.) and reduces everything to an annual return. This makes it possible to compare projects that initially have little in common. It is therefore an indicator that is above all financial, an aid to decision-making before any investment.

Projects with a high internal rate of return are often considered by management and also by shareholders as having the highest priority.

See also: investment, TSR

International Standard Organisation (ISO)

In its own words, ISO is an independent, non-governmental international organisation with 165 national standards bodies as members.

To date, ISO has published more than nineteen thousand International Standards in a wide range of fields, from agricultural and construction standards to the latest developments in information technology, mechanics and medical devices.

Widely known are:

-   *ISO 26000* (2010): Guidelines for social responsibility
-   *ISO 31000* (2009): Risk management; Principles and guidelines
-   *ISO 14001* (2004): Environmental management systems; require-ments and guidance for use
-   *ISO 9001* (2015): Quality management and quality assurance

opposite: there is none
see also: compliance, non-conformity

Investment

It is the purchase by an organisation of goods and services that will be used several times in the course of the productive activity.

A distinction is made between:

- *tangible investments* (purchase of machines, buildings, etc.);
- *intangible investments* (purchase of software, training, marketing, research and development, etc.).

Investments are thus expenditures that make it possible to maintain or increase the production potential of the enterprise, i.e. its technical capital.

Therefore, the expression *investing in one's future* does not make sense. If it did not, it would not be an investment.

opposite: disinvestment
see also: amortisation, asset, depreciation

Investment funds

An investment fund is a company that invests capital in business projects corresponding to its specialities. Investment funds can be part of banks, financing organisations, but also owned by individuals; their capital is most often pooled.

They are often specialised in one sector. Capital can be provided at the start of a company's life: this is called venture capital. If a company calls on the investment fund to finance its development, the financing activity is called development capital.

see also: managed funds, hedge funds

Investor

An investor is a person or organisation that provides money to a company with the aim of making a profit. Typically, the investor's capital or tangible assets are invested in shares, real estate and funds, but also in shares in companies, especially in start-ups and often also in the form of convertible loans.

Start-ups and new companies are most often dependent on the financial input of an investor, but longer established companies also receive investments, often in several rounds of financing or to achieve a turnaround.

Many young entrepreneurs confuse *investors* with good Samaritans; the investor expects a profit, never forget that... even though the investor wants you to call him a *business angel*.

opposite: *all those who do not invest*
see also: *business angel, start-up, turnaround*
see also (optional): *Luke 10:25-37*

J - K

Jobs (not Steve)

"I don't want yes-men around me. I want everyone to tell the truth. Even if it costs them their jobs." *Samuel Goldwyn*[21]

Job description

A job description is an internal document within the organisation that specifies the requirements of the job, its duties, responsibilities and the skills required to perform a role. The description should be detailed enough for the person reading it to understand not only the scope of the job but also the corporate culture in which the job is performed. It is important, however, to leave some room for individual discretion to the employee to whom the job description is addressed.

In most countries there is no legal requirement for a job description or even how to write it. The job description is a double-edged sword: with it, both the employee and the employer know what they want from the role but risk being constrained by the description. Conversely

---

[21] US-American film producer. He was involved in the founding of well-known film studios such as United Artists and Metro-Goldwyn-Mayer.

without it, there is the risk of an unworkable role. In this second case, Oprah would surely whisper again.

"When you don't know what to do, do nothing." *Oprah Winfrey*[22]

opposite: letter of dismissal
see also: jobs, management system

Joint venture

It is the association of two or more companies cooperating with each other to achieve a common goal. In more concrete legal terms, a joint venture is an undertaking planned by two or more companies which are legally and economically independent of each other, sharing both the management tasks, the responsibility and the economic risk. In this sense, the joint venture is created and the companies involved continue to exist independently and are shareholders in the joint venture.

As the English term joint venture originates from the idea of daring together, some corporate communications will prefer the expression of *formalising a strategic alliance*.

Joint ventures are very often like marriages; they fail most of the time when goals are not clear, communication between partners is poor or because of financial problems. Finally, joint ventures also fail when the partners have been on the market for too short a time.... rings a bell?

"Don't do it, you are too young!" *my mother*

opposite: celibacy (?)
see also: partnership

Knoster's chart

Prof. Tim Knoster[23] has extensive experience in teacher professional development.

This renowned pedagogue has published a chart corresponding to the changes in attitude and the ability of children to change and learn. This concept is not only applicable to the student, but also and especially to the company that wants to manage complex changes and communication in general.

---

[22] American talk show host, television producer, actress, author, and philanthropist.

[23] American pedagogist. Professor at the McDowell Institute for Teacher Excellence in Positive Behavior Support in the College of Education.

Knoster's chart[24] indicates that to make a change successful you need 5 elements: Vision, skills, incentive, resources, action plan.

If you are missing any of these elements, change cannot take place and your action will have an immediate and negative effect on the people you are trying to reach.

- If the vision is missing, the team will be confused
- If the skills are missing, the team will be anxious
- If the incentive is missing, the team will resist to change.
- If the resources are missing, the team will be frustrated
- If the action plan is missing, there will only be a false start

see also: change management, transformation, vision

KPI (Key Performance Indicator)

A KPI is a measure that allows companies to evaluate the performance of an area. KPIs are often lumped together with metrics, although there is a difference between the two terms:

- KPIs are linked to an objective. Decision-makers use them to ensure that strategic and operational objectives are met.
- Metrics express the raw quantitative value of a variable or parameter. A metric becomes a KPI if it is linked to a target value.

As KPIs allow the comparison of the effectiveness of organisations, it is possible to identify a typical list of those used by actors in the same sector of activity:

- *In marketing and sales*: percentage of loyal customers, satisfaction rate (or net promoter score), % market penetration, % increase in turnover, profitability per customer
- *Particularly for digital*: bounce rate for a website, number of unique visitors, number of page views, number of new visitors, average duration of visits, conversion rate for an email campaign, average shopping cart value, shopping cart abandonment rate
- *In finance*: return on investment (ROI), return on equity, growth rate
- *In human resources*: turnover rate, absenteeism rate, employee satisfaction, % of trained employees

---

[24] Knoster T., *A framework for thinking about systems change*, p. 95-112.

—   *In logistics*: stock-out rate, service rate, on-time delivery rate

opposite: KRI
see also: goal, objective, OKR, target

KRI (Key Result Indicator)

Do not confuse KRIs with KPIs (key performance indicators), they are not the same thing!

KRIs report on the results of many activities, they are retrospective and inform about what happened. KRIs measure the effect of business activities but ignore the cause.

KPIs do not measure objectives; KRIs do. KPIs track single actions or activities, while KRIs track the aggregate results of many actions.

opposite: KPI
see also: goal, objective, OKR, target

Kübler-Ross curve

Elisabeth Kübler-Ross[25] defined in 1969 a curve of grief in 5 stages: shock/ denial, anger/ fear, sadness/ depression, search for meaning/ trying/ acceptance and finally serenity/ new strengths. To these 5 stages, Kübler-Ross linked appropriate forms and tones of communication in order to accompany the person griefing.

Many economists, managers and academics have adopted the Kübler-Ross curve and applied it directly to the psychological condition

---

[25] Swiss-American psychiatrist, a pioneer in near-death studies.

of employees in a changing organisation. Change is the end of one thing and the beginning of another, just as in the case of griefing.

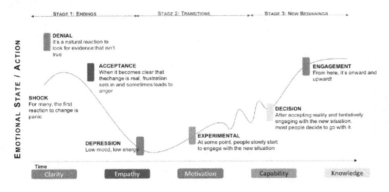

Kübler-Ross curve with emotional states and ways of communication[26]

While the Kübler-Ross curve, also known as the change curve, is often shown in companies, the forms and tones of communication are often omitted or unknown. This is a pity, because this is where the power of Elisabeth Kübler-Ross' work is to be found.

opposite: none
see also: change, fatigue (change), transformation

---

[26] Own representation

L

Leader

Social networks and management books will tell you everything and certainly anything about the difference between a leader and a manager. Well-known and lesser-known people will quote the definition of a leader and as a result not to confuse it with a manager.

Finally, many blogs, articles and comments of all kinds will tell you that you have to be a leader and not a manager.

This glossary will be no exception to the rule; here is my definition: a leader is a manager you want to follow. Nothing more, nothing less.

opposite: manager (internet says)
see also: manager

Leadership

Make an educated guess as to what it might be!

"People who enjoy meetings should not be in charge of anything." Thomas Sowell[27]

---

[27] American economist, social theorist, and senior fellow at Stanford University's Hoover Institution.

opposite: management (internet says)
see also: management

Legacy

Legacy is what is inherited. In business, it is mostly what the previous management left you. The term legacy is usually used in a negative sense to indicate that the heritage of the previous management is a burden that the current management would gladly do without.

opposite: current, new, future
see also: LCF

Leveraged buy-out (et al.)

LBO (Leveraged Buy Out) is a financial operation consisting of the purchase of a company through a debt mechanism. The funds borrowed to finance the LBO are repaid from the profits of the target company.

There are generally 4 forms of leveraged buy-out:

- *LMBO* (leveraged management buy-out): if the buyers are senior managers of the company, it is a leveraged management buy-out
- *LBI* (leveraged buy-in): if the investors are all external to the company being acquired, it is a leveraged buy-in
- *BIMBO* (buy-in management buy-out): If the buyers are both external investors and managers of the acquired company, this is called a Buy-In Management Buy-Out
- *LBU* (leveraged buy-up): if the shareholders subsequently plan to merge the company with another, this is an optimised accumulation

see also: acquisition, merger

Liquid asset

A liquid asset is any type of asset your organisation holds that can quickly be converted to cash while still keeping its market value.

opposite: fixed asset
see also: asset, current asset

Liquidity

Liquidity should be understood as a switch that can convert the organisation's assets into cash. In other words, it means how fluid your ability is to access the money the organisation holds.

opposite: illiquid
see also: cash, liquid asset

Loan

„I need a dollar, dollar a dollar is what I need (hey, hey)" *Aloe Blacc*[28]

A money loan is the handing over of a sum of money to a borrower who has to pay it back, for a fee (usually interests).

see also: interest

Loss carryback

This is a tax technique worthy of an H.G. Wells[29] book: it is a *machine* that allows current tax losses to be set against past taxable profits. The result is a tax refund.

opposite: loss carryforward
see also: loss carryforward, tax

Loss carryforward (LCF)

Loss carryforward refers to an accounting and tax practice whereby companies use their net operating losses of the current year to offset net operating profits of subsequent years, in order to reduce taxes due in those future profitable years. This practice can be used by individuals, corporations or any other form of organisation subject to income tax.

Depending on the country and jurisdiction, losses carryforward can be set off against future as well as past profits (loss carryback). The amount of the offset may also be limited or unlimited.

opposite: loss carryback
see also: EBT, tax

---

[28] Egbert Nathaniel Dawkins III aka. by his stage name *Aloe Blacc* is an American musician, singer, songwriter, record producer, and philanthropist.

[29] English writer. His most notable science fiction works include *The Time Machine* (1895) and *The Invisible Man* (1897).

Love money

Love money is a concept that originated in the United States in the 1960s and corresponds to equity capital contributed to the creation of a company by family, friends, etc., in order to help the creator. In return for these contributions, the investors become partners in the company created.

The sums contributed to the start-up may be in the form of a donation or a loan between individuals. They are accompanied by advantageous repayment conditions.

The advantage of love money is that the lender helps someone close to him or her to start a business and the entrepreneur obtains funds on favourable terms. The disadvantage is that friendship becomes a money matter.

„Lend money to an enemy, and thou will gain him, to a friend and thou will lose him." *Benjamin Franklin*[30]

see also: investment, start-up

---

[30] American printer, publisher, writer, scientist, inventor and statesman. As one of the founding fathers of the United States, he participated in the drafting of the United States Declaration of Independence and was one of its signatories.

M

Managed funds

A managed fund is the pooling of money from different investors into a single fund that is invested and controlled by a professional investment manager.

When investing in a managed fund, the investor does not own any direct shares in the companies in which the fund invests but is only allocated a number of units.

see also: funds, hedge funds

Management

10 people are paid to do what 6 people would do better with three when two are not there. This is the impression that many employees have when they think of management.

It is therefore the duty of the manager to understand the function (see definition below) so as not to fall into the trap described above.

see also: manager (read it right now!)

Management system

The management system is the process set up by a company (or an organisation) to achieve its quality policy and objectives.

The ISO 9000 standard provides a description and ISO 9001 translates them into requirements to be implemented.

We can identify 7 keys to the success of a management system:

- Customer orientation
- Leadership (for ISO: commitment at the highest management level)
- Involvement of personnel
- Process approach
- Improvement
- Evidence-based decision making
- Stakeholder relationship management (including *return of experience*)

see also: ISO, process, standard

Manager

According to Luther Gulik[31], management is defined by the 6 generic functions: Planning, Organising, Staffing, Directing, Coordinating, Reporting and Budgeting (POSDCORB).[32] The person performing these functions is therefore a manager.

Professional social networks are full of great articles about the manager versus the leader and vice versa. Let's ignore all that: if managers in organisations were able to fulfil the six functions defined by Gulik, companies would already be better off.

opposite: leader (internet says)
see also: leader

Marketing

Marketing can be defined as the analysis of consumer needs and the set of actions used by organisations to influence consumer behaviour.

The most well-known types of marketing that exist are

---

[31] American political scientist, Eaton Professor of Municipal Science and Administration at Columbia University, and Director of its Institute of Public Administration, known as an expert on public administration.

[32] Gulik L., *Notes on the Theory of Organisation*, p. 13.

- *Direct marketing*: which consists of communicating information about a product, service or company directly to customers (emails, letters, telephone, etc.)
- *Relationship marketing*: all the marketing actions that a company can implement in order to create a privileged relationship with its prospects and customers. In other words, relationship marketing aims to establish a direct, continuous and personalised relationship and close communication with each of its customers and, on a larger scale, with its prospects.
- *Transactional marketing*: focused on the transaction, i.e. the act of buying. It is the opposite of relationship marketing.
- Strategic marketing: including all the orientations and decisions relating to a company's marketing strategy.
- *Product marketing*: research, promotion and sale of a product to a customer. It is a branch of marketing that aims to find the right customers for a particular product and to create a compelling case for those customers.
- *Operational marketing*: referring to all the techniques and means used to achieve marketing objectives. The decisions taken in operational marketing are applied in the short or medium term. They are constantly renewed to keep pace with market developments. Operational marketing is often contrasted with strategic marketing.

see also: market segmentation, USP

Market segmentation

Market segmentation consists of dividing the market into homogeneous groups of consumers, according to quantitative or qualitative criteria. A market segment is therefore a group of consumers with similar needs and purchasing behaviour. The aim is to better understand the market and then choose the sub-group(s) of customers that will constitute the target.

In theory, segmentation allows you to improve your competitiveness, brand awareness, customer loyalty and communication. If segmentation affects so many factors in your business, it automatically affects your profitability.

However, excessive segmentation is bad for business. Many companies have gone too far and many specialists have forgotten that segmentation has a higher cost in terms of stock, loss of economies of scale, more complex production, communication and distribution.

Car manufacturers have made the break with this and have reduced the number of models as well as the choice of colours. And with some brands, the choice of options is almost non-existent.

The same is true of retail sector, where new types of shops have appeared, such as large food stores that have decided to offer only a limited choice in order to lower their prices.

opposite: market aggregation
see also: business plan, strategy

Market share

The market share of a service or product is the ratio of the sales of that product or service by one company to the total sales of the same product or service in the market by all groups in the market.

But what happens when a product or service is disruptive and does not yet have a market? A disruptive innovation will create a new market and make the old one obsolete. However, the risks associated with this kind of innovation are high because the success of the product is entirely dependent on the acceptance of the change.

The best modern example of a failed disruptive innovation is Google Glass. These glasses, with extremely advanced features, were a huge fiasco for Google because the public was not ready for such a revolution. The idea was certainly great but the change in consumer behaviour was perhaps too high or even too ahead of its time.

"A great product will survive all abuse. Google Glass is a great product. How do I know? Every person I put it on (I did it dozens of times at 500 Startups yesterday) smiles. No other product has done that since the iPod." *Robert Scoble*[33]

opposite: marketless
see also: marketing

Merger (& Acquisition)

The term "mergers and acquisitions" (M&A) refers to the combination of two business entities into one. A merger is when two companies form

---

[33] American blogger, technical evangelist, and author.

a new entity. In the case of an acquisition, one company buys another and integrates (if possible or desired) its activities with its own.

The aim of a merger or acquisition is to create a new entity that is more efficient and effective than the two previous companies were on their own.

opposite: spin-off
see also: horizontal integration, vertical integration

Millenials

Millenials is a term used to refer to Generation Y.

opposite: Generation X
see also: Y, X, Z Generation

Mission statement

The mission statement is the single, synthetic text written and communicated by an organisation in which it specifies its mission around four elements: its purpose, its values, its field of activity and the priorities among its stakeholders. It is central to its strategic process and is the result of a participatory process.

The mission statement is mainly used to motivate employees and to make strategic and financial decisions. It has an important role in human resource management.

see also: strategy, vision

Motivation

Motivation is the set of factors determining the action and behaviour of an individual to achieve a goal or carry out an activity. It is the combination of all the reasons, conscious or not, collective and individual, which incite the individual to act within a team. Motivation is exogenous, whereas the inspiration that drives the individual or group to act is endogenous.

Motivation is one of the challenges of the managerial function, whereas inspiration, although endogenous, can only be instilled by a person that the group is ready to follow (a leader?).

The psychologist Abraham Maslow[34] defined motivation in the light of the hierarchy of human needs.

---

[34] American psychologist who developed a hierarchy of needs to explain human motivation.

He established a theory of motivation in psychology that includes a five-level model of human needs, often represented as hierarchical levels in a pyramid. From the bottom of the hierarchy upwards, the needs are: physiological (food and clothing), security (job security), love and belonging (friendship), esteem and self-actualisation.

The needs at the bottom of the hierarchy must be satisfied before individuals can attend to the needs higher up. Many occupational psychologists and human resource specialists use this hierarchy of needs to develop employee motivation programmes.

opposite: inspiration
see also: inspiration, management, trust

Motivation and variable remuneration

The multi-generational organisation does not sound the death knell for the variable elements but it requires on top of all, that the entrepreneur and his/her team go back to basics in putting the accent on the motivation cycle.

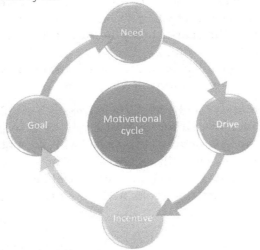

Motivational Cycle[35]

For the science of psychology, the motivational state is known of being made up of four different states that take place in each one to push the person to each action. Each action is initially initiated based on a

---

[35] Own representation.

specific need. The need urges the person to act. The positive results achieved by the actions act as an additional motivation that urges the person to achieve his or her goal. But the individual can never stop after reaching a certain goal, and it goes on and on.

The organisation must instill inspiration in using the motivational cycle. How does it work?

- *Need*: the organisation must make clear that there is a need. A need is lack or deficit of some necessity. For any goal directed behavior, need is the first condition or stimulating factor.
- *Drive*: this is the second step towards achieving goal. Drive can be defined as the state of tension or arousal produced by need. For example, the need for office space may generate more digitalisation or some other form of surface use. (e.g. desk sharing). Drive acts as a strong persistent stimulus to push an employee towards its goal. It is the state of heightened tension leading to restless activity and preparatory behavior.
- *Incentive*: Not only the variable elements are meant here but also, in our example about the office space, getting a better working environment. The motivated behavior is directed towards incentive and getting closer to the incentive provides satisfaction of the aroused drive.
- *Goal*: Once the goal has been completed, the employee is again ready for another goal-motivated behavior.

The use of the motivational cycle applied to each employee gives meaning, even a different one for each of them, to an organisation's variable compensation structure. Everyone will be entitled to a differentiated motivation but will receive a similar variable element base. By applying this method, the organisation will be able to increase the number of its intrinsically motivated employees aka "inspired makers".

opposite: no pay, no work!
see also: inspiration, manager, remuneration

N

Nano-manager

"It doesn't make sense to hire smart people and tell them what to do; we hire smart people so they can tell us what to do." *Steve Jobs*

The nano-manager is the extrapolated form of the micromanager. The latter, who wants to control everything and is never satisfied with the work done by his subordinates, has been transformed into a nano manager with the help of digital technology. Nano-managers are probably people who want everything done exactly their way, but who provide little explanation, support, help or advice.

They need to control everything because they don't trust their teams, and often the feeling is mutual. Nano managers slow down processes and projects by demanding that all decisions go through their desk.

A nano-manager:

- forbids you to make decisions;
- demands a daily activity report;
- regularly complains about everything and everyone; and
- does not pass on any know-how or share his or her experience.

opposite: laissez-faire

see also: manager, pointy-haired boss (PHB), process

Negative equity

In principle, equity must be at least equal to half of the share capital. If this is not the case, e.g. if the equity falls below 50% of the capital contributed by the partners, the equity is said to be negative. In other words, the value of the company is considered (in theory) zero or negative, because the amount of its debts becomes greater than the amount of its assets. The reason for this is that the accumulated losses do not allow the company to retain half of its share capital.

opposite: positive equity
see also: equity, debt equity ratio

Non-conformity

In any organisation, a product or service offered must meet requirements specified in documents usually called *specifications*.

The organisation also has to deal with quality management requirements, external customer requirements, in a broader sense, requirements from stakeholders.

This results in three types of non-conformity:

- product non-conformities which lead to non-conforming products or services;
- quality management system non-conformities that no longer allow the organisation to be guided and controlled with regard to quality; and
- non-conformities that confirm non-compliance with the requirements of interested parties.

"Skipping: the ultimate display of non-conformity" *Jessi Lane Adams*[36]

opposite: conformity
see also: ISO, specifications, standard

---

[36] Jessi Lane Adams is an extensively quoted person on the Internet. After a long search, it turns out that she or he does not exist at all. He or she should therefore be quoted in this book as well, as a solid source of thoughts.

Non-executive director

Non-executive director is a part-time board member who is not an employee of the company and who takes part in the planning, strategy and policy of an organisation but not in its operations.

Non-executive director is usually appointed to ensure the independence and balance of the board and to ensure good corporate governance. He or she may also be appointed for his or her prestige or because of his or her particular experience, contacts or knowledge.

opposite: executive director
see also: director, governance, strategy

Non-verbal communication

Non-verbal communication refers to all elements of an exchange that are not directly related to speech. The discipline is studied in psychology, based on the principle that our bodies sometimes send out stronger messages than our words. The attitude of an interlocutor who is lying can thus be in total contradiction with his or her words.

According to a rule called the "3V rule", based on studies published in 1967 by Professor Albert Mehrabian[37], only 7% of communication is verbal (the meaning of words). 38% of this communication is vocal (the intonation and sound of the voice), 55% is visual (facial expression and body language). Therefore, 93% of communication is non-verbal.

Non-verbal communication is so important that it has its own expressions in many languages and cultures: in Japanese *reading the air*, in English, French or German *between the lines.*

This form of communication is unconscious; the manager must therefore be aware of his vocal and visual communication if the message is to reach the right person.

opposite: verbal communication
see also: communication

---

[37] American Professor Emeritus of Psychology at the University of California, Los Angeles. Although he originally trained as an engineer, he is best known for his publications on the relative importance of verbal and nonverbal messages.

O

Objective

It is the result towards which the organisation's action tends. It is not to be confused with the goal.

Indeed, the objective is the means to achieve the goal, to arrive at the finality. The aim is a set of statements, derived from one or more ideas, which will be expressed in the form of a goal to be achieved. The objective will be what has been chosen to achieve this goal.

"The objective is to achieve the target defined by the goal" *Unknown*

opposite: aimless
see also: goal, target

Objectives and key results (OKR)

OKRs or 'Objectives and Key Results' are a methodology for setting objectives to help teams set measurable ambitions. While most companies set goals, only a few employees report being aware of them and say that their company sets and communicates them effectively. OKRs are a simple and effective tool to communicate:

I *will (objectives) measured by (key results).*

Key results are the indicator for measuring progress towards the goal. Key results can be quantitative or qualitative (more difficult to measure).

see also: KPI

Offshore account

Stop thinking that an offshore account is something illegal, because it is not! In many countries, there is no legal prohibition against owning or opening an account outside your country of residence and depositing money in it. However, beware: most countries require that they be declared to the tax authorities.

So, in summary, there are two illicit reasons for opening an offshore account: not wanting to pay tax and wanting to hide assets elsewhere than in your place of residence.

opposite: domestic account
see also: tax

Onboarding

Welcome aboard!. If your onboarding process is limited to this sentence, your organisation has an obvious problem nowadays.

The onboarding process is crucial for companies because the start of a new employee has a great influence on further development and productivity. It decides whether the newcomer feels welcome, enjoys working with them and integrates well into the team and the company. It is not about rushing new employees into work as quickly as possible. They should feel much more welcome and get to know the company. Integration into the company structure, culture and processes is crucial. A well thought-out and designed onboarding process is an exciting and important experience for the further course of the relationship between employee and employer.

Don't hesitate to sign up your Head of HR for an internship at the neighbouring primary school in the first grade. The onboarding process for new employees is not that distant from that in first grade.

opposite: lay off
see also: human resources, process

Operating (profit / loss)

The operating result is an intermediate management balance that details the company's income and expenses over the past accounting period. It is referred to as an operating profit when its income is greater than its expenses, or an operating loss when its income is less than its expenses.

see also: profit (& loss)

Operating expenses

Operating expenses are disbursements made by a company in order to achieve a certain turnover. The formula operating expenses is characteristic of the industrial sector.

opposite: income
see also: overheads

Operations

Everything that happens within a business to make it work and make money is collectively called "business operations".

By inference, anything that occupies the company but is not part of the value chain for generating profit, e.g. a social day such as an employee Christmas party, should not be called an operation.

see also: business

Opportunity

The word opportunity refers to a favourable time or opportunity to do or seize something.

It is therefore important to be aware of opportunities in any field and to analyse them to determine the most suitable option.

In general, we can talk about

- work or professional opportunity, which refers to the chances that a person has to improve their work situation.
- work opportunity that can be the possibility of a promotion, a job offer or the proposal to start a new business or project.

In business you will often hear about

- the opportunity section which is the area of a shop where items are sold at a lower price than usual; and
- the opportunity cost, which is the cost of investing available resources in an economic opportunity, thereby setting aside other available alternative investments. In other words, the

opportunity cost relates to what an economic agent gives up when making a decision.

opposite: threat
see also: SWOT (analysis)

Order to cash

The term Order to Cash is used to describe the processes related to the activities of the orders from to the payment by the customer. The term originates from the era of large ERP projects such as SAP, Oracle, AS400, etc.

The activities included under the term Order to Cash are generally

- *management of quotations*: receipt of a customer request, issue of a quotation and/or a commercial proposal, possibly validation workflow before sending to the customer;
- *processing of customer orders*: receipt and registration of the order, internal transmission and supply/shipping of the product and/or service; and
- *customer invoices*: issue of the invoice, reminders on late payment, registration and reconciliation of the payment

Always keep in mind that this process is critical for the organisation as it affects the customer on one hand and finances your business on the other. This process must be the centre of attention for the manager.

opposite: purchase-to-pay
see also: digitalisation, ERP, processes

Ordinary shares

Ordinary shares are one of the two most common types of shares.

In fact, the majority of shares issued are in this form. Ordinary shares are an ownership interest in the company and are entitled to a share of the profits (dividends). Investors hold one vote per share e.g. to elect members of the board of directors, which oversees major decisions made by management.

The second most common type of shares are preferred shares.

opposite: no shares
see also: board of directors, preferred shares

Organic growth

Organic growth, also known as internal growth, results in an increase in the means of production, distribution and research created thanks to the company's internal resources (human, financial and technical resources, etc.). In short, organic growth is based on a strategy of self-development that can be quantified by an increase in the number of customers and/or by an increase in the average turnover generated with each customer.

opposite: inorganic growth
see also: turnover, merger & acquisition

Organisation

An organisation is a social group of interacting individuals with a collective goal, but whose preferences, information, interests and knowledge may differ: a company, a public administration, a trade union, a political party, an association, etc.

Each of these organisations has a management that respects the common rules of its function.

opposite: individual
see also: chart (organisation)

Overheads

Overheads on ongoing business costs that are not related to labour, materials or third-party costs that are charged directly to customers (for example, shipping costs).

In simple terms, these are costs that are not associated with the creation or production of your goods or services.

Normally, overheads are paid on an ongoing basis - whether or not the business benefits. Knowing your overheads is essentially important for budgeting your organisation and also for pricing your products or services to make a profit. The most common overhead costs are rent, insurance and utilities.

see also: costs of sales, operating expenses

"Over my dead body"

The expression "Over my dead body" originates from the character trait of the Great Pyrenean dog breed. If a farmer's sheep were injured, the Great Pyrenean dog was usually found dead as well, killed while trying to protect the flock.

The expression today is often used outside English-speaking countries as a threat, which can be translated as *if you want to do it, you'll have to kill me first*, implying that if you do it, the person you are talking to will kill you.

You've been warned, haven't you?

opposite: please do so.
see also: communication, management

P

Partnership

A partnership is a formal agreement between two or more parties to manage and operate a business and share the benefits.

However, let us not forget the existence of the so-called 'silent partner', where one party does not participate in the day-to-day operations of the business but contributes capital and shares in the profits. In addition to contributing capital, an effective silent partner can benefit a business by giving advice when called upon, providing business contacts to develop the business and mediating disputes between the other partners.

The most common types of partnership are:

- *general partnership*: agreement between partners to establish and run a business together;
- *limited partnership*: a form of partnership similar to a general partnership except that a limited partnership must have at least one GP and at least one limited partner. The limited partners are only liable up to the amount of their investment.

- public-private partnership: partnership of purpose between the public sector and private sector companies.

see also: joint venture

Patent

A patent protects a technical innovation, i.e. a product or process that provides a technical solution to a given technical problem. The invention for which a patent may be obtained must also be new, involve an inventive step and be capable of industrial application.

Many innovations are patentable, provided they meet the criteria for patentability and are not expressly excluded from protection by law.

Some inventions are not patentable but can be protected by other means, such as copyright or design rights.

However, there is evidence that filing and registering a patent does not guarantee making money from it.

opposite: public knowledge
see also: innovation, trade secret, USP

People Management

Whereas until the end of the 1980s personnel management was often limited to the administrative side (contracts, salaries, contributions, holidays, etc.), today it is a more complex task. Competence support and development, resource planning, talent selection and development, etc. are now at the centre of personnel management.

See also: human resources, human capital, jobs

Philanthropy

Philanthropy is the performance of selfless acts for the good of others, inspiring a tradition of giving and sharing that is essential to the quality of life.

Philanthropy certainly includes monetary donations, but also includes donations of goods, volunteering, community involvement, social entrepreneurship, responsible purchasing, etc.

But then how can we not dissent when talking about philanthropy and business. Giving money clearly contradicts the commercial and profit-making objectives of the company. It is also important to differentiate between philanthropy and sponsorship; in the latter, the return on investment is certainly quite intangible but it is recognised by all. In the case of philanthropy, the benefit will most often be found in the values it supports. The values honestly lived by a company are part of its value to employees (employer branding) but also in its positive impact on its socio-economic environment. Today, the company must be a player that cares about its environment in all its forms.

The other side of the coin is the biased use of the system. Many academics agree that companies that invest in the common good generally expect a return on their good deeds. This sounds fair, but a darker side has emerged over the past decade, both in theory and in practice. Some companies use philanthropy as a marketing tool, for a variety of purposes, from increasing the popularity of the CEO to manipulating local public opinion.

opposite: misanthropy
see also: environment, green washing, marketing

Pirates

"Why join the navy if you can be a pirate?" *Steve Jobs*[38]

Pointy-Haired Boss (PHB)

In common language, pointy-haired people are known for their extreme qualities that distinguish them from computer professionals and are often considered out of touch with technology.

The pointy-haired boss was originally a character in the *Dilbert* comic strip created by Scott Adams[39]. This boss is characterised by micromanagement, incompetence, ignorance of his surroundings and unnecessary use of buzzwords, yet he retains power in the workplace.

To call someone a pointy-haired boss is to say that they are at their most incompetent.

„In Japan, employees occasionally work themselves to death. It's called Karoshi. I don't want that to happen to anybody in my department. The trick is to take a break as soon as you see a bright light and hear dead relatives beckon." *Pointy-Haired Boss*[40]

---

[38] US-American entrepreneur. As co-founder and long-time CEO of Apple Inc. he is considered one of the best-known personalities in the computer industry.

[39] American artist and creator of the Dilbert comic strip and the author of several nonfiction works of satire, commentary, and business. For many seasoned managers, Scott Adams is the god of snark at meetings.

[40] Strip published on Tuesday November 02, 1993, https://dilbert.com/strip/1993-11-02

opposite: competent manager
see also: incompetency, manager, nano-manager

Post-merger integration (strategy and operations)

It describes the period after the transfer of shares (share deal) or assets (asset deal) has been completed within the framework of an M&A transaction and the processes that take place during this time, with which the legally completed connection between acquirer and target is also materially implemented.

This period can range from a few months to several years, depending on the complexity of the transaction. In numerous studies, post-merger integration (PMI) is presented as an evolutionary process that is primarily driven by the acquirer or by the management of the combined entity. The primary goal here is to use the potential opened up by the M&A transaction in such a way that the enterprise value or, not least, the shareholder value of the acquirer or the combined entity is increased.

see also: merger & acquisition, integration

Powerful

"Being powerful is like being a lady. If you have to tell people you are, you aren't." *Margaret Thatcher*[41]

Being powerful means having the ability to control or influence people or things.

opposite: powerless
see also: leader, KPI

Preferred shares

Preferred shares, unlike common shares, represent a degree of ownership in a company but do not generally carry the same voting rights. With preferred shares there is usually a guarantee of a fixed perpetual dividend to the holder. This is different from ordinary shares, whose dividends are variable and mostly never guaranteed. Another advantage is that in the event of liquidation, preferred shareholders are

---

[41] Aka. *The iron Lady*, British stateswoman who served as Prime Minister of the United Kingdom from 1979 to 1990 and Leader of the Conservative Party from 1975 to 1990.

paid before ordinary shareholders (but still after debt holders). Preference shares can also be redeemable, which means that the company has the option to buy the shares from the shareholders at any time and for any reason (usually for a premium).

As such, some academics consider preferred shares to be more like debt than equity.

see also: equity, ordinary shares

Price

Price is the value of a good or service and is most often expressed in monetary units (Euro, Yen, etc.). In other words, the price is the value that an individual is willing to pay for the transfer of a good or service.

The theory is that the price reflects the balance between supply and demand. Thus, when supply is high, the price is very often lower and vice versa. Pricing is therefore linked to scarcity, availability of the good or service and demand. The rarer a good is, the higher its price and vice versa.

Cheap cars are rare, so rare cars are cheap. Is that right?

opposite: free
see also: cash, investment

Private equity

Originally, private equity, or unlisted equity, consists in buying shares in unlisted companies. This investment is made directly or through companies or funds. As the shares are not listed on the financial markets, it is often said that private equity allows investment in the so-called real economy.

Meanwhile, the business of private equity is to invest in companies, usually with the aim of growing their business and/or improving their performance. Private equity funds today invest in companies that have one of the following profiles:

- unlisted growth companies
- *orphan companies* or underdeveloped divisions of large companies
- listed companies whose share price is undervalued or whose growth potential could be better exploited by private shareholders.

see also: managed funds, investment

Process

The term process refers to a system of activities that uses resources to transform inputs into outputs. Processes are all the contributions made by the people in an organisation to deliver the promise to the customer.

Many people in business are so proud of their processes that they forget to continuously improve them as the rule of a good management system requires. They mistakenly think that the process should be trusted.

Trust the Process is a slogan used by fans of the Philadelphia 76ers[42] in the NBA, although it has since become popular elsewhere in sports and culture. Made up during a difficult time for the team, it essentially means *things may look bad now, but we have a plan in place to make them better.*

opposite: spontaneous
see also: action plan, hope, standard

Profit & Loss (P&L)

The profit and loss account is a mandatory accounting document for companies and is prepared at the end of each accounting period. The profit and loss account presents an objective description of the company's expenses and income during the accounting period in question.

Expenses include, for example, operating expenses and financial expenses. Income will include operating income and financial income. The profit and loss account will make it possible to draw conclusions from all the company's financial operations.

This account complements the balance sheet, which is the image of the economic and financial performance for the accounting period.

opposite: none
see also: EBITDA, purpose

---

[42] American professional basketball team based in the Philadelphia metropolitan area. The 76ers compete in the National Basketball Association as a member of the league's Eastern Conference Atlantic Division and play at the Wells Fargo Center.

Project

A project is a set of activities organised in phases or stages and forming the management unit for achieving a defined and precise objective.

"How does a project get to be a year late? One day at a time." *Fred Brooks*[43]

Project Management

In theory, project management is project management and project leadership.

-    *Project management* is the set of management tools necessary to conduct the project in terms of technical performance, quality, cost control and time control. This is the methodology.
-    *Project leadership* has the task of setting objectives and providing the means adapted to the size of the project for its optimal implementation. These objectives are strategic, political, organisational and human.

The project responds to a need and is deployed within a specific framework: defined objectives, ad hoc team, means used, etc. The project has a beginning and an end. Project management covers all the organisational methods used to carry out the project.

In practice, the human aspect of a project within an organisation is strongly based on the ability to lead, inspire and motivate participants throughout the project to achieve success.

The project manager must therefore be both an orderly person and someone who can sense the changing moods of the group and individuals. The project manager's communication will therefore be crucial to success.

Most of the failed projects were not due to technical means but to weak project execution and poor communication.

opposite: project mismanagement
see also: communication, manager, change fatigue

---

[43] American computer architect, software engineer, and computer scientist, best known for managing the development of IBM's System/360 family of computers.

Purchase to pay

The term Purchase to Pay is used to describe the processes related to purchasing activities, from the order to the payment of the supplier. The term originated in the era of large ERP projects such as SAP, Oracle, AS400, etc.

The activities included in the term Purchase to Pay are generally the following

- *purchase requests*: issuing a requirement, workflow and/or procedure for validating the request, supplier selection steps; and
- *purchase orders*: issuing the order to the supplier, receiving confirmation, receiving delivery (material or services); and
- *supplier invoices*: registration, reconciliation, timely payment to the supplier.

While purchase to pay includes all the usual criteria for process optimisation (quality, costs, deadlines), another criterion should not be overlooked: compliance.

It is very important to ensure that purchases are made in accordance with the company's rules, in particular that not everyone buys just anything from anyone at any price. For example, that preference is given to purchasing from catalogues or referenced suppliers, that only approved parts or products are ordered, etc.

opposite: order to cash
see also: digitalisation, ERP, processes

Purpose

Purpose is the reason why something exists. In the context of an organisation or business, projects, groups and departments often have names that are far removed from their purpose. It is more important to look at what they do.

Stafford Beer[44] coined and frequently used at conferences the word "POSIWID" (the purpose of a system is what it does) referring to the commonly observed phenomenon that the de facto purpose of a system is often at odds with its official purpose.

---

[44] British theorist, consultant and professor at the Manchester Business School. He is best known for his work in the fields of operational research and management cybernetics.

"According to cyberneticians, the purpose of a system is what it does. This is a basic principle. It is a simple fact, which makes it a better starting point in the search for understanding than the usual attributions of good will, prejudices about expectations, moral judgement or simple ignorance of circumstances."[45]
Stafford Beer

---

[45] Stafford Beer, (2002), "What is cybernetics?", *Kybernetes*, Vol. 31 Iss: 2, pp. 209 - 219.

Q

QHSE

Quality, Health, Security, Environment: QHSE. The sequence of letters has no legal significance, but rather is a cultural feature of each organisation.

Whereas HSE is a responsibility that falls directly on the management and engages its civil and sometimes criminal liability, quality (in the sense of management quality) is more flexible in its constraint. The certification of the latter is not necessarily a proof of quality in practice and vice versa.

However, QHSE remains an essential function for all quality management - with or without production - because, just like the legal compliance rules, it is not a trivial matter!

opposite: would you seriously like to work in a place without QHSE?

see also: certification, environment

QM (Quality Management)

It is as important as HSE and thus deserves its own paragraph.

Quality is not just a matter of common sense, tools and techniques. It is a mindset, a process of change and a method that involves everyone in the company. It requires a collective awareness and a permanent evolution of the organisation's internal culture.

Since quality is the ability to meet the implicit or explicit requirements of customers, it is not what we think we put or recognise in a product or service, but what the customer finds there and what he is prepared to pay for. Everything else is wasteful and has no value.

The key principles of quality management are those underlying the ISO 9001 (quality management system) standard and the EFQM excellence model[46].

- *Results orientation:* the purpose of the company or organisation is to maintain and improve its overall capabilities and performance to satisfy its customers as well as other stakeholders (staff, shareholders, suppliers, partners, community, etc.).
- *Customer focus:* The company or organisation depends on its customers and needs to understand their current and future needs in order to develop their satisfaction.
- *Leadership and consistency of vision:* Managers set the direction and are involved in achieving the objectives. This creates the environment for development and improvement.
- *Involvement of staff:* this allows for the optimal use of staff 'skills', building trust and accountability. These areas are fundamental to the service (managing the customer-organisation interface through customer-facing staff).
- *Process approach:* To be effective, activities and their related resources are managed as a process.
- *Continuous performance improvement:* this is a permanent objective of the organisation.
- *Factual approach to decision making:* Action decisions are based on data analysis.
- *Mutually beneficial relationships with suppliers:* the company (or organisation) and its suppliers are independent. Mutually beneficial relationships allow each to "create value".
- *Responsibility towards the community:* the company or organisation acts as a "good corporate citizen" (ethical behaviour), takes care to prevent nuisance and directs its

---

[46] EFQM (European Foundation for Quality Management) is a non-profit organisation domiciled in Brussels and established in 1989 to increase the competitiveness of the European economy.

activities towards the conservation and sustainability of resources.

opposite: no quality management
see also: ethic, non-conformity, HSEQ

Quo vadis?

From Latin: where are you going to?

This is the central question that every manager must ask himself every morning. If the management of an organisation does not know where it is going, how do you expect stakeholders to follow or, worse, trust them?

Answering this question clearly and in a structured way every morning enables managers to manage their function well.

„The pessimist complains about the wind; the optimist expects it to change; the realist adjusts the sails." *William Arthur Ward*[47]

---

[47] William Ward (1769–1823) was an English pioneer Baptist missionary, author, printer and translator. He wrote a lot of very motivational thoughts.

RACI matrix

The RACI matrix (or table) is a tool for determining the roles and responsibilities of each actor in a project or process. The name of the matrix (RACI) is an acronym with each letter corresponding to one of the specific responsibilities:

- *Responsible*: does the job
- *Accountable*: is liable to get the job done
- *Consulted*: involved before the action is taken/decided
- *Informed*: involved after the action is taken/decided

It is a two-dimensional table with:

- *In rows*: activities, tasks, actions, deliverables, etc.
- *In column*: actors, designated as people, organisational entities, functions, jobs, teams, etc.

The RACI matrix comes in many variations, allowing for more or less granularity as well as more or less comprehensive consideration of a project's timeline.

An example is the IPCARSED matrix:

- *I* is for Initiation

- *P* is for Preparation
- *C* is for Check/ Consultation
- *A* is for approval
- *R* is for Release
- *S* is for Supervision
- *E* is for Execution
- *D* is for Distribution

See also: Knoster's chart, project

Receivables

A receivable is the amount of money that a company must collect from a customer.

Thus, a creditor is a person who has a claim on another person, the debtor.

opposite: payables
see also: accountant

Responsible

The "responsible" in business is mainly the one who does the work. Not to be confused with the person who is accountable nor with the one who is liable.

see also: accountable, RACI

Remuneration

For the managers, remuneration is above all a strategic element with less negligible consequences on the result and policy of the company than on the quality of the work of the teams.

Main pilar of the renumeration, the wage is the consideration for the work performed by the employee and corresponds to a certain job level or qualification. Wages are freely determined at the time of hiring subject to compliance with certain legal or contractual rules that may set minimum wages.

The challenge for all managers will be to build a compensation system to retain and inspire teams while ensuring the flexibility required by any organisation.

That's why a holistic approach to employee compensation elements in light of the organisation's demographics will make your company an attractive or unattractive environment.

Remuneration can be synthesized in 5 distinct elements which together form the levers that allow the leader to guide his/her teams to achieve the strategic goals of his/her organisation.

- A fixed element: the salary (called basic salary), bonuses (seniority, family, etc.), the 13th month, etc.
- A personal variable element
- A corporate variable element
- A deferred item
- Social benefits

While the fixed element remains linked to factors external to the organisation, such as the job market, employee qualifications, hiring negotiations, variable, deferred and fringe benefits are the levers available to the employer to motivate, if not inspire its employees.

The right balance with social benefits (flexible working hours, workplaces at employees' discretion, the right to bring one's pet to the workplace, etc.) depends on the type of employer, the type of job and especially on the target the employer is aiming at.

At the origin of any decision concerning remuneration, the question must be asked whether or not it supports the company's strategy; not only from a results point of view but also from the organisation's social policy viewpoint.

Money is not always at stake. Money only has an ephemeral value in the employee satisfaction index. It is mainly about retaining the good people who make up the economic strength of the organisation. The adage is that the employee leaves his manager before leaving his employer: money is only a trigger but not a reason.

Retention

The term retention is about binding employees to the company through certain measures. Within the business field of human resources, it is also known as employee retention. The elaboration of these measures is attributed to retention management.

The employer must be the bearer of the message given to its employees to retain them; inspiration, perspective, passion, challenge, values and many other points are the drivers of employee retention. If all of this is no longer present in the company or if the *mermaids' song* of the competition is too tempting during a difficult transformation of the employer, then organisations often use the retention bonus as a last option. The last chance tool for employee retention is the retention bonus, i.e. a loyalty bonus that is paid for and when the respective employee remains with the company until a certain point in time.

opposite: turnover
see also: churn rate, employer branding, turnover

Revenue

Let's not look for complicated definitions of what is simple: *Revenue* is the money brought into an enterprise by its business activities.
Stop thinking that revenue is the same as turnover, because it is not! Revenue is the total amount of money coming in, or received:

- *revenue is a cash flow concept*: it refers to a real financial flow, therefore often expressed with taxes (if applicable in the activity jurisdiction),
- *revenue is not always equal to turnover*: there may be a time lag between invoicing and collection,
- *revenue is compared with expenses* (outgoing cash flow).

opposite: broke
see also: turnover

Risk

A *risk* is an event whose random occurrence is likely to cause damage to people or goods or both.
A risk is therefore an event, it is not personified. An employee cannot therefore be a risk, only his or her action.
One of the roles of the manager is to anticipate risks by classifying them in order of probability and consequences so that they do not occur or, if they are unavoidable, that they have the least possible impact and, above all, that they do not recur or become over-accidents.
There are four types of risks:

- *High probability, low impact*: if these things happen, you can cope with them and move on. However, you should try to reduce the likelihood that they'll occur.
- *Low probability, low impact*: you can often ignore them.

- *Low probability, high impact*: you should do what you can to reduce the impact they'll have if they do occur, and you should have contingency plans in place just in case they do.
- *High probability, high impact*: These are your top priorities, and are risks that you must pay close attention to.

Some people call this role of the manager *risk management*, but Stafford Beer's vision of risk management must be taken into account.

opposite: planned event
see also: non-conformity, risk management

Risk Management

"You cannot manage risk; you just can be ahead of it." *Anthony Stafford Beer*

Return on Investment (ROI)

ROI is a financial indicator that measures the profitability of a project, an investment, an action, a marketing campaign, etc. It can be summarised as follows: "If I put this amount of money into the project, how much will I get back?" In other words, what is the benefit obtained in return for the costs incurred?

ROI is expressed as a percentage (rate of return on investment) or as a value: *ROI = (Revenue - Investment costs) / Investment costs*.

The only negative point, but not the least, is that it is not always easy to know precisely all the costs to be taken into account. This is particularly true when indirect costs are involved, which are difficult to measure. In this case, cost accounting is a valuable support in allocating a set of expenses to cost centres efficiently.

see also: IRR, TSR

Servant leadership

To put it bluntly, servant leaders have the humility, insight and courage to recognise that they can learn from people at all levels of an organisation. They see their responsibility as a leader as increasing the confidence, capability, ownership, autonomy and responsibility of their people. They are humanists before being servants.

The concept, or management philosophy, of servant leadership became widely known with Robert Greenleaf's 1971 essay[48]. In it, he takes up several concepts from both Western and Eastern philosophy with Laozi[49] also arguing that the leader should ask himself what he can do for others.

opposite: directive manager
see also: humanist manager

---

[48] US-American manager, founder of the Servant leadership movement and the Greenleaf Center for Servant Leadership.
[49] Chinese philosopher and writer who lived between 6th and 4th century BC.

Shareholder value

The concept of shareholder value was first defined in 1986 by the American economist Alfred Rappaport. According to this concept, the value of a company is measured by the market value of its shares.

The fundamental valuation factors of shareholder value that should always be included in strategic considerations are

- Sales growth and profitability
- Tax rate
- Net investment in fixed and current assets
- Duration of a competitive advantage
- Cost of capital

The shareholder value strategy is basically about maximising value by making decisions for the shareholders. The aim is to extract the greatest possible value for the investors involved.

see also: stakeholder, TSR

Silos (working in)

With the advent of digital technology, not only have our consumption patterns changed, but also our entire structural environment, starting with the organisation of work. While siloed work is tending to disappear, or at least organisations are working to make it disappear, hotbeds of resistance, often led by members of Generation X, are still alive and kicking.

Working in silos means that each department works on its own specialties without worrying about the others. To give just one example: It is as if your process engineering department works on the projects sold without agreeing, step by step, with the sales department about the customer's needs and requirements. In fact, in a company that operates in silos, there is no sharing of information or resources, and no cross-functional communication, i.e. departments communicate little or nothing with each other. The hierarchical system is very present and the management is pyramidal, i.e. employees are relieved of responsibility and their autonomy and creativity is curbed.

This type of organisation generally leads to duplication of tasks, loss of time and often financial loss. In short, it is an obsolete way of operating that is detrimental to the overall performance of the company and is not adapted to the digital transformation that we are currently experiencing.

Moreover, generations Y and Z are bringing a new wind and are not ready to work in silos. The need to understand their actions and to have a vision of the company as a whole is key for them.

In practice, it is not easy to break out of a traditional hierarchical organisation. It involves changing the culture of the company as well as the working methods. However, as it is often the case, a return to the basics of management will help to eliminate silos in five steps:

1. *Communicate a common vision and goals*: Typically, in silo organisations, employees focus on their individual and departmental goals and lose sight of the overall corporate objectives. Often, some departments even feel they are in competition with each other, and rather than collaborating, they will, in the worst case, intentionally withhold information to put their "rivals" in trouble. The value chain, punctuated by the organisation's processes, is the central pillar of the organisation. If this value chain is not conscious and recognised by each and every employee, you will not be able to break down the silos.

2. *Promote collaboration between teams*: To break down organisational silos, you need to encourage teams to work and interact together on pre- defined common goals.

3. *Create teams around projects*: To work efficiently and succeed in all your projects, set up multidisciplinary teams, for example with a member of each department involved in the project (technical, marketing, sales, product, etc.), from the very beginning of a project.

4. *Use collaborative tools*: In today's digital age, there are many tools and applications available that promote team collaboration and facilitate communication and the sharing of ideas and information. These tools are ideal for breaking down organisational and geographic silos, allowing employees to easily work together, regardless of their location.

5. *Train your teams to work collaboratively*: Finally, training is an excellent way to succeed in effectively and sustainably „desilotate" your business.

opposite: co-working
see also: organisation chart, team

Social enterprise

Social enterprises are companies that place the interests of people and the planet ahead of shareholder gains, or at least at the centre of the values they share with their shareholders. These companies are driven by a social/environmental mission and reinvest their profits in creating positive social change.

In a social enterprise, the notion of "performance" must be understood in a broader sense than just financial profitability. Concepts such as IRR, ROI and particularly TSR need to be revised to correspond to the activity and teleology of the social enterprise.

opposite: is there any?
see also: KPI, CSR

Social Media

The term social media refers to digital platforms accessible via the Internet (web and applications) and allowing their members to establish or integrate networks of friends or professional contacts and to participate in the life of these networks through the provision of tools and interfaces for presentation, communication and interaction.

In view of their success in terms of audience and usage, social media are essential media or supports for marketing and advertising. This use is made in particular through community management and the purchase of advertising space.

Access to these social media is mostly free for those who only want to use them in their basic version. As the economic performance of the platforms is based on the analysis of data related to the behaviour of members and the placement of advertisements to members, it has become clear that the product sold by social media is the members. The service is therefore not provided to the members but to those who place messages and advertisements for profit or socio-economic-political purposes.

"Random social media tactics lead to random results. You need a strategy"
Stephanie Sammons[50]

opposite: clubhouse
see also: communication, customer, marketing

---

[50] Stephanie Sammons is a Certified Financial Planner, LGTBQ financial advisor, sing-song writer, speaker and bestseller author. She is also a (step-)mom of two.

Speak-up

Speaking up is the easiest and at the same time the most difficult thing in an organisation. Often managers do not know how to react to employees who speak up.

There are usually two reasons for this:

- Managers, especially mid-level managers, do not have enough room for action within their organisation to make changes as a result of their employees' speaking up. So these managers somehow stifle the possibility to express themselves in order not to be confronted with their impossibility to act in the short term.
- In the case where managers accept the demands and want to implement them, they often come up against the fact that they lack sufficient long-term visibility for the implementation of the expressed demands.

In other words, a culture of speaking up means empowering managers to take action, but also communicating long-term goals and possibilities. Without this paradigm shift among middle level managers, there will be no speak up culture in the organisation.

"I can't remember me telling you, correct me if I'm wrong." *Anonymous manager*

opposite: timid
see also: change, communication

Specification

A specification is the translation of the customer's subjective needs into a precise description of what the product should do. It is a feature that defines an aspect of the final product.

Three recurring problems with specifications can be identified:

- specifications change throughout the development process
- specifications are decided after development has been completed
- there are no specifications.

opposite: no specification
see also: customer

Spin-off

The spin-off of a company is the operation whereby a company transfers its assets and liabilities to two or more pre-existing or new companies. It thus leads to the dissolution of the split company. In return, the partners of the company will receive shares in the recipient companies.

This is a fairly rare operation, but it does exist. Because of the enthusiastic split-ups that occur in times of crisis, it is important to be familiar with this expression, which can be useful during a group reorganisation.

opposite: merger
see also: asset, merger

Stakeholder

The stakeholder concept refers to a vision of the company based on negotiated governance, i.e. where the question of shareholder profit and its increase are not the main objectives to be achieved. It is a model of governance in which the interests of the company's stakeholders are paramount, as they are the ones who will ensure its prosperity.

This model therefore stands in opposition to the shareholder value principle, which focuses on optimising the shareholder's return on investment.

opposite: me, myself and I
see also: shareholder value

Standard

A standard is a reference document, a rule established to define or evaluate a product, a working method, a quantity to be produced, the amount of a budget.

Norms or standards must be visual, simple and formalised in order to be understood by all.

"The standard you walk past, is the standard you accept." *Lieutenant General David Morrison*[51]

see also: certification, ISO

---

[51] Australian Army Chief (2011-2015)

Start-up

This term is used to describe an innovative new company with high growth potential and speculation on its future value. However, the start-up must first go through a phase of experimenting with its market and its business model.

In the meantime, the term startup is used in everyday language to define a young company in a technological field, with or without high growth potential.

see also: business plan, unicorn

Strategy

A strategy describes the ways and means a company chooses to achieve its goals. It shows how the company intends to be successful in competition.

The strategy is built around seven important elements:

- Vision - Without the vision there is no strategy.
- Mission - Clarify who you are and why.
- Core Value - The values of a company.
- Market Analysis.
- Long-term goals.
- Targets for each year.
- Action Plan.

"The biggest risk is not taking any risk... In a world that is changing really quickly, the only strategy that is guaranteed to fail is not taking risks." *Mark Zuckerberg[52]*

see also: goal, Knoster's chart, value

Success

"Success is going from failure to failure without loss of enthusiasm." *Winston Churchill[53]*

Success is a subjective notion that is usually measured by KPIs set in advance but which for obvious communication and political reasons are often set after the fact.

---

[52] US entrepreneur and philanthropist. He is the founder and chairman of the board of Facebook Inc.

[53] Considered the most important British statesman of the 20th century. He was Prime Minister twice - from 1940 to 1945 and from 1951 to 1955.

Supplier

A supplier is someone who provides a good or service to a company on a regular basis. It is just as important for a company to manage its supplier relationships well as its customer relationships.

Indeed, profit is born in the purchase.

opposite: customer
see also: customer, payables

Supply Chain

The supply chain consists of the supply, production and distribution stages of the goods. It is divided into different flows:

- *physical flows*: the movement (transport) and storage of goods.
- *information flows*: a company creates a huge database which it stores on its servers. This database is a collection of information. It contains the goods offered, the different participants in the process, the strategies adopted, the resources made available, etc.
- *financial and administrative flows*: all the documents and transactions that circulate between the various players in the supply chain (partners, suppliers and subcontractors, as well as within the company). These flows include order processing, control of the delivery schedule, control of orders and control of payments and management reports.

The main issue is therefore the management of flows.

Supply chain should not be confused with the logistics chain, which refers to the management of the warehouse, internal and external transport flows, supplies and the final delivery of products to customers.

opposite: logistic chain
see also: purchase to pay

Sustainability

Let's be committed! here is a subjective definition of the word:

Sustainability is the concept that defines the need for transition and change that our planet and its people need to live in a more equitable, healthy and environmentally friendly world.

The purpose of sustainability is to define viable models that bring together the economic, social and environmental aspects of human activities. These three areas must therefore be taken into account by organisations and individuals. The challenge of sustainability is to find a coherent and sustainable balance between these three aspects. In addition to these three pillars, there is a cross-cutting issue that is essential to the definition and implementation of sustainability policies and actions: good governance.

opposite: transitory
see also: environment, greenwashing, governance

T

Takeover

A takeover is a restructuring process that involves a change in the majority shareholder. The acquisition of a small share of the capital (usually less than 25%) is in principle insufficient to influence the structures of the company concerned. It is therefore necessary to cross the threshold of 50% of the capital, which will enable effective control to be exercised by controlling the decisions which are the competence of the board of directors.

see also: board of directors, merger & acquisition

Talent management

Talent management is a branch of human resources that aims to attract, develop and retain high-potential profiles that enable the company to significantly increase its competitive advantage. Talents are employees whose know-how (skills, expertise) and interpersonal skills (aptitudes) exceed the average of all employees.

Talent management is based on an initial planning stage aimed at defining the concept of talent and the KPIs.

„CFO: What if we train them and they leave? CEO: What if we don't and they stay?" *Unknown*

see also: human resource, human capital

Tax

Tax is a sensitive political issue in all companies. However, let's remember why taxes are there. Tax has three purposes:

- *To finance* the functioning of the state, schools, civil servants' salaries, roads, etc.
- *To influence* taxpayer behaviour to achieve the government's strategy (e.g. granting a tax allowance for the installation of photovoltaic panels on the roof helps to accelerate the energy transition).
- *To redistribute* wealth among the population. This part does not always seem to work, given the regular demands of citizens in all countries.

The utopia of an economic environment without state funding is not acceptable. The Principality of Monaco or the United Arab States have little or no taxation but finance themselves, one by gambling in the casino and the other by oil which still flows freely.

Taxes must therefore be accepted for what they are: a compulsory outlay for the organisation which, in the event of profits, reduces the result that can be distributed to shareholders.

"In this world nothing can be said to be certain, except death and taxes." *Benjamin Franklin*

see also: financial statement, profit

Team

Together Everyone Achieves More.

opposite: individual

Teleworking

Whatever your view on mobile working, this is a big trend. Remote working was already on the rise before COVID 19. In the United States, for example, it has more than doubled since 2005 to reach 4.7 million workers. If you look at recent headlines, this would be an easy and smooth transition. The pandemic crisis has nevertheless revealed that the digitalisation of the workplace was not accomplished at all and that some small or midsize companies have even been forced to make employees and work mobile.

And yet, this shift to a utopian future seems questionable: take the example of IBM, which decided to abandon teleworking several years ago, because it hampered innovation and collaboration. A lot of managers in several companies already can highlight other challenges and difficulties linked to teleworking. And if people don't take a smart approach to telework, they risk a deterioration in their working lives.

In the pro-telework camp, there are promises of reduced travel time, increased quality time at home, productivity gains and a better work-family balance. Sceptics counter that this flexibility has to be paid for. They worry about the loss of social interaction, the nuance and sense of community - and the possibility of reduced productivity.

After a teleworking honeymoon period of the confinement and social distancing, working at a distance is now causing a feeling of isolation for 25% of the employees.

As the one told me, we are not all professional of self- motivation. In the office as in the teleworking, the managers are responsible to motivate the employees beyond the natural self-motivation that each of us is supposed to have. Nowadays, one cannot be pro-telework or sceptical; managers must keep a regular contact with employees, communicate more and dispatch meaningful work. Only those who will individually take care of their people in making their management intent transparent, their critics fair and who will communicate with integrity, will gain the trust of their employees and be able to create talented teleworkers.

Employers will have to pay a particular attention to departments or divisions which are usually performing well and in the times of teleworking are suddenly underperforming. In this particular case, it might be that the manager in charge is not able to manage teleworkers.

At the end, the real challenge is the ability of managers to deal with teleworkers for the benefit of the company purpose and that, beyond the fact that there are talented and untalented teleworkers.

opposite: office work
see also: manager

Tender

Tender is a procedure whereby a potential buyer asks different suppliers to make a costed commercial proposal in response to the detailed formulation (specifications) of its need for a product, service or provision.

Winning a tender is the aim of any commercial proposal. Elvis understood this well.

"Love me tender, love me sweet, never let me go." *Elvis Presley*[54]

opposite: direct sale
see also: competition, price

Trade secret

Trade secrets can be reduced to three main ingredients:

- It has commercial value and provides a competitive advantage.
- Its owner keeps it secret, does not disclose it publicly.
- It is subject to reasonable safeguards within the company.

When combined, these characteristics give rise to a right that can be defended in court in the event of unauthorised disclosure, theft or misuse.

There is one downside: although the company may have recourse against the discloser, once the secret is out, it is no longer a secret!

opposite: public knowledge
see also: intellectual property, patent

Total Shareholder Revenue (TSR)

Total shareholder return (TSR) is an indicator of financial performance, showing the total amount an investor receives for an investment - in particular a shareholding. To arrive at its *total*, usually expressed as a percentage, TSR takes into account capital gains and dividends but also special dividends, stock splits and even warrants. However it is calculated, TSR means the same thing: the sum of what a unit or share has given back to those who invested in it.

see also: shareholder value

---

[54] American singer, musician and actor. He is considered as one of the most significant cultural icons of the 20th century and is also known as the "King of Rock and Roll". And yes, he passed away.

Trust

Authenticity, sincerity, transparency and fairness are the social fundamentals of humanist enterprise and are the social basis of trust.

Trust can be broken down like a tree whose main branches are character and competence. Starting from the premise that a company in its trade does not need to prove its competence, then the essence of trust is built around character.

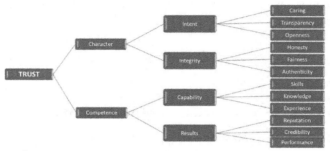

Component of trust[55]

On the one hand, the *intent* which is demonstrated by:

- *Caring*: to look after the well-being of the employees and the organisation;
- *Transparency*: being clear about the motivation for all decisions; and
- *Openness*: accepting and receiving the opinions and ideas of all employees.

On the other hand, the *integrity* demonstrated by:

- *Honesty*: being honest and forthright in all interactions;
- *Fairness*: acting without bias, discrimination or injustice; and
- *Authenticity*: being consistent and sincere in word and deed.

Trust is one of the essential elements of an effective team. The humanist manager must ensure that trust exists within the team, between the team and the manager, between the organisation and its stakeholders.

opposite: distrust
see also: communication, team

---

[55] Steve R. Covey, Speed of trust

Transformation

Stop thinking change and transformation are the same, because they are obviously not!

Whereas change in a business context involves the planning and implementation of specific actions that will impact on individual business units or the company as a whole, transformation involves a multitude of interconnected actions relating to an entire socio-cultural system. The goal of transformation is to replace the old with the new, to redefine business models and to reinvent the company - in short, a much more visionary company.

Transformations are more unpredictable than change projects, as they usually impact several business units. The risks of a transformation are also higher, as even management does not always know (including in terms of results) where the journey will take them.

opposite: status quo
see also: change, strategy, vision

Transformational merger

A transformational transaction (or merger) is one that changes the very nature and operations of a business. Examples include the acquisition of new markets, channels or products, the sale or merger with another company, or any other transaction that may have a lasting effect on the business. The most sophisticated form is the merger of two companies which then form a new entity with a new and different value proposition.

see also: acquisition, merger, transformation

Turnaround

Business turnaround refers to a set of practices aimed at reversing this trend, at 'turning around' a situation that is not going well in favour of the company, with a view to revitalising the business and safeguarding jobs, even if this approach sometimes involves a wave of economic layoffs.

Beyond restructuring, far from being systematic, a turnaround plan can also include reorganisation, cost rationalisation and the search for new financial resources

The naughty analysts will say that it is the last measure of a shareholder before turning everything around.

opposite: status quo
see also: strategy, transformation

Turnover

Stop thinking that revenue is the same as turnover, because it is not!

Turnover is the sum of sales of products and goods invoiced over the period under consideration. It is therefore a fundamental performance indicator for the company, since it gives a precise idea of the volume of activity:

- Turnover is established in exclusive of tax,
- It does not include financial income, extraordinary income or changes in stocks,
- Turnover is the sum of invoices issued, even if the money has not been collected.

opposite: partly broke
see also: revenue, receivables

U

Unanimity

„I don't think leadership demands *yes* or *no* answers; I think leadership is providing the forum for making the right decision, which doesn't demand unanimity." *Arthur Ochs Sulzberger jr.*[56]

opposite: disagreement
see also: shareholder, leadership

Unicorn

Aileen Lee[57] was the first person to use the word unicorn[58]. This American venture capitalist conducted a study in 2013, showing that less than 0.1% of the companies in which venture capital funds invested reached valuations of more than 1 billion dollars. Eager to give its

---

[56] Arthur Ochs Sulzberger is a US-american journalist. He was the chairman of the The New York Times Company from 1997 to 2020, and the publisher of The New York Times from 1992 to 2018.

[57] American venture capital investor. She coined the often-used Silicon Valley term unicorn in a TechCrunch article *Welcome To The Unicorn Club: Learning from Billion-Dollar Startups*

[58] https://techcrunch.com/2013/11/02/welcome-to-the-unicorn-club/?guccounter=1

analysis the best publicity, it looked for a selling term to describe these nuggets.

She found the perfect word "unicorn": something rare, dreamy and heroic fantasy related, a culture that is totally compatible with geek culture.

With over 600 companies in the world meeting the unicorn criteria[59], I don't know if they shouldn't change their name.

opposite: start-up (?)
see also: advantage, USP

Unwilling manager

Gender note: I have never met a female unwilling manager. After asking around, among my fellow partners and some clients, no one could give me a female example. That is why this paragraph is written in the use of the masculine gender.

He was not very efficient in the management of his department, but this was not so obvious as he did everything himself, delegated very little and his unique unit was always successful. However, as soon as he was appointed head of the division, his hesitancy or even immobility in management became evident and his reluctance to commit, delegate or become more involved in more complex organisational and operational structures became a problem for the smooth running of the company.

The unwilling manager must, however, be able to do an effective job and stay on track, so if you are unlucky enough to have such a manager, how do you help him and, more importantly, the division he leads to succeed? Keep in mind that what they need is support and encouragement, not criticism. Here are some tips for working with unwilling managers in individual situations:

- *Vision:* Ask them how they see the future of their division. Make sure you listen actively and do not pass judgement. They probably have some idea of what success looks like. Once they have formulated a clear and focused vision, help them communicate this vision to people throughout the division and the organisation and publicly support their vision for the future.
- *Decision-making:* Help them identify decisions they do not like to make. These are usually the day-to-day operational decisions. Team up with them and express your willingness to lead the

---

[59] https://www.cbinsights.com/research-unicorn-companies

implementation of difficult decisions. This will probably require you to partner with other team members.

- *Management:* Because of his aversion to conflict, he needs to be reassured and helped to be realistic about the real consequences of difficult conversations. It is not that he is unaware of the need to have these conversations, he just doesn't know how to deal with the difficult issues.

All of these would require the employee to take a risk and start acting more like a colleague of the manager than a subordinate. However, you may find that these managers appreciate your help and begin to rely on you to help lead and focus the organisation. By combining their intelligence and understanding of the business with your ability to execute, you could make a very good team... if HR does not fire him before!

opposite: competent manager
see also: coaching, leadership, manager

USP (Unique Selling Proposition)

The USP is a marketing concept made in the USA which explains the success of some advertising campaigns in the early 1940s. The main objective of these campaigns was to convince prospects to switch to a different brand of product, through unique selling propositions. The term comes from a pioneer in television advertising: Rosser Reeves[60] of Ted Bates & Company.

USP is based on three criteria:

- *the proposition*: recipients must read into it the message: "Buy this product, and you will receive this benefit(s) in return."
- *its uniqueness*: the proposition must be one that competitors do not or cannot offer. It must be unique, either through brand originality, unique claim or if it offers a fresh angle.
- *its strength*: the USP must be strong enough to sell. This includes selling to prospects and attracting new customers.

„M&M's melt in your mouth, not in your hand" *Rosser Reeves*

opposite: real world competition
see also: advantage, differentiation, value proposition

---

[60] Rosser Reeves (1910-1984), American advertising executive and pioneer of television advertising, he was creative director at the advertising company Ted Bates & Co. from 1940 until 1965.

Utility

Utility measures the total level of satisfaction of an individual when consuming a good. The level of utility refers to the point at which one is happy to consume a good.

There is no objective scale for measuring utility. The value that an individual attributes to a good has no value as such, it simply allows an individual to rank the consumption goods available to him in order of preference.

Marginal utility refers to the level of satisfaction provided by the last unit of the good that has just been acquired.

Marginal utility is always decreasing: the more the quantity consumed increases, the less intense the need to consume more of the good.

The additional satisfaction provided by the acquisition of an additional unit decreases as one accumulates units of the good, until the point of saturation where the marginal utility is zero. Beyond this point, marginal utility is negative and total utility falls. But a rational consumer, of course, would never pass this point and so marginal utility is considered to be decreasing, never negative.

In my empirical study, I found that the marginal utility of my chocolate consumption is never negative.

opposition: frustration
see also: benefit

V

Value chain

The notion of a value chain defines the enterprise as a chain of activities transforming *inputs* into *outputs* ultimately purchased by consumers. These activities are, moreover, interconnected.

The combination of the different processes and their interactions generate value in the eyes of customers. Value is therefore not limited to the firm as such, since it also includes the relationships it has with its partners (subcontractors, distribution channels, etc.).

see also: order to cash, purchase to pay, supply chain

Value proposition

The value proposition is the element at the heart of your marketing strategy that helps convince the consumer to buy your product or service. It expresses the advantages or benefits, real or expected, that the offer will bring to the customer, by solving one of his problems for example, or by satisfying a wish or an aspiration.

Defining the value proposition is a fundamental step in developing a relevant marketing approach.

The value proposition must be unique. It allows you to distinguish yourself from your customers and from your competitors.

Usually, it emerges from a six-step process:

- Identify who your product or service is aimed at
- Find the problem your offer addresses
- Define the advantages of your offer over the competition
- Write a unique and clear value proposition
- Validate the value proposition and its assumptions
- Expressing your value proposition

opposite: proposing commodities
see also: differentiation, USP

Venture Capital

Venture capital is an investment in the equity of unlisted companies that are going to be created or have just been created and that have an innovative project or high growth potential, but for which debt financing is often not appropriate or difficult to find.

Venture capital covers two categories:

- *seed capital:* directed towards the actual creation phase of the company; and
- *creation capital:* in the post-creation phase.

see also: love money, investment funds

Vertical Integration

Vertical integration can be upstream or downstream. Upstream integration means that the company starts to produce what it previously bought from the supplier.

Downstream vertical integration means integrating the activity of intermediaries in order to eliminate them and thus sell directly to the customer.

see also: horizontal integration

Vision

The vision is an overall picture of what an organisation wishes to become at the end of a previously agreed planning horizon.

Beware! A vision is not an objective or a list of objectives to be achieved.

It is a thousand times more than that, it is an operating concept whose genius is to contain everything that participates in the history of a company, from its start to its end, from its founding idea, its catalytic energy (what it wants to do) to the completion of the project.

And not only does the vision concept contain the ingredients of what will make the future history of the company, but it puts them in dynamic relation to each other in order to generate the movement of implementing the original intention, giving life to the original idea, and realising the perceived project.

A company's vision must succeed in bringing together the *why* of the company and its *what for*. In this respect, it is the drawing, the plan of the path between the initial impulse and the target, it is the path to follow between the causality and the consequence.

opposite: blind flight
see also: mission statement, strategy

W

Webpage and website

Stop thinking a webpage and a website are the same because they are not!

A webpage is what makes a website work. It is a single document adapted to your web browsers (Google Chrome, Internet Explorer, Mozilla Firefox, Safari, etc.).

A website is a collection of web pages under a single domain name. These webpages will now be identified with the common domain name.

opposite: leaflet
see also: communication

Why?

This is the most important question to ask. As a manager if you can't answer why your company exists, why it is a player in its market and why you do what you do, you need to stop right now and find the answer. If the answer is not found within the next hour, then ask yourself why you are there!

"People don't buy what you do; they buy why you do it. And what you do simply proves what you believe" *Simon Sinek[61]*

opposite: why not
see also: USP, vision

Working capital

Working capital is a key indicator of the financial equilibrium of a company. It corresponds to the difference is the difference between a company's current assets, such as cash, accounts receivable and inventories of raw materials and finished goods, and its current liabilities, such as accounts payable. Thus, it measures the quantity of stable resources available (which are not used by fixed assets) to finance the company's current operating expenses.

In other words, it is the amount of money constantly available to the business to meet its cash outflows while waiting for its cash inflows.

see also: DSO, DPO

Work-life balance

Talk of work-life balance is often synonymous with a predictable dispute. Work-life balance means a balanced relationship between work and private life. The aim is to bring private interests into harmony with the demands of the working world in a healthy and balanced way. After all, concentrating your personal commitment on one area at a time also limits your quality of life.

It seems that the world is divided into two types of people:

- those who see the work-life balance as an ideal to be achieved because they see two worlds clashing - the world of work and the world of their private life; and
- those who see the work-life balance as nonsense invented by psychologists in need of novelty. For them, since work is the nature of man (since no other animal works on its own) then it is part of life: there is no balance to be found within a single element.

---

[61] britisch-US-amerikanischer Autor und Unternehmensberater.

My advice: choose your side and engage in this endless discussion. You have everything to lose, and you will not change anything.

opposite: life without work
see also: inspiration, motivation

X – Y – Z

X (Generation)

They were born between 1961 and 1981 and are distinguished by the fact that they are the inventors and champions of the work-life balance.

Like all generations, to understand them one must consider the environment in which they formed their character; the easiest way to do this is to identify their purpose in life, the central object of their generational culture, their usual communication tools and their preferred means of communication.

The cultural environment of the X generation is defined through:

- *Purpose in life*: work-life balance (whatever you think it is)
- *Central object*: a PC (on which they could tinker)
- *Usual communication tools:* emails and short-message texting
- *Preferred communication tools:* emails

opposite: baby-boomers
see also: millenials, Y-generation, Z-generation

Y (Generation)

Also named *Millennials*, they were born between 1982 and 1996 and are characterised by the fact that they are the inventors and champions of freedom and agility.

Like all generations, to understand them one must consider the environment in which they formed their character; the easiest way to do this is to identify their purpose in life, the central object of their generational culture, their usual communication tools and their preferred means of communication.

The cultural environment of the Y generation is defined through:

- *Purpose in life*: freedom, flexibility, agility, change (whatever you think it is)
- *Central object*: smartphone and tablets (on which they could change every two years)
- *Usual communication tools:* short message texting, social media
- *Preferred communication tools:* online (whatever they do) and mobile phone

opposite: X generation
see also: Z generation

Year to date (YTD)

The year-to-date (YTD) is the period between the first day of the calendar year and the current date. It is generally used to calculate the investment return of a security or the income of a company up to the current date.

see also: financial statement, project

Yield

Yield is the term for earnings generated and realised on an investment over a specific period of time, expressed in a percentage.

Yield includes price in- and decreases as well as any dividends paid, calculated as the net realised return divided by the principal amount (i.e. amount invested).

see also: TSR

Z (Generation)

They were born between 1997 and 2011 and are characterised by the fact that they are the inventors and champions of the green and securised environment. They grew up during a recession and in the time of global warming

Like all generations, to understand them one must consider the environment in which they formed their character; the easiest way to do this is to identify their purpose in life, the central object of their generational culture, their usual communication tools and their preferred means of communication.

The cultural environment of the Z generation is defined through:

– *Purpose in life*: living in a secured and green world

– *Central object*: they are technoholics. They love nano-computers, 3D-printers, driverless vehicles,

– *Usual communication tools:* mobile devices and internet of things (IoT)

– *Preferred communication tools:* videocalls (zoom, facetime, etc.), snapchat

opposite: nothing compares to Z
see also: environment, X generation, Z generation

Zombie

Zombies are unprofitable, indebted companies that only survive on low interest rates. The term zombie company dates back to Japan's "lost decade" in the 1990s.

Economists generally define a zombie as a company that has been in existence for at least ten years but is unable to cover the cost of servicing its debt with its profits over a long period of time and whose stock price is lagging behind.

One explanation lies in the attitude of the more fragile banks, which prefer to renew their loans to such companies rather than write them off.

More generally, these zombie companies have survived thanks to the fall in interest rates which has not encouraged them to restructure their activities.

Perhaps more seriously, the existence of these zombie companies lowers the total productivity of companies and thus the overall performance of an economy.

Even worse, their existence prevents healthier companies from fully developing, as they manage to divert some investment and employment.

"Anything is possible until your heart stops beating." *The Walking Dead*[62]

opposite: healthy company
see also: bankruptcy, insolvency

---

[62] Father Gabriel Stokes *in The Walking Dead – Season 7, Episode 12.*

Bibliography

Adams D., *The Hitchhiker's Guide to the Galaxy: The Illustrated Edition*, New York 2007.

Adams S., *The Dilbert Principle: A Cubicle's-Eye View of Bosses, Meetings, Management Fads & Other Workplace Afflictions*, New York 2014.

Beauvoir (de) S., *The Second Sex (Vintage Classics)*, New York 2014.

Beer S., *Brain of the Firm*, New York 1995.

Christensen C., *The Innovator's Dilemma: When New Technologies Cause Great Firms to Fail (Management of Innovation and Change)*, Brighton 2015.

Covey S., *The Speed of Trust*, Salt Lake City 2008.

Dante A., *The Divine Comedy: Volume 1: Inferno*, Oxford 1961.

Greenleaf R., *The Servant as Leader*, South Orange 2015.

Gulik L., *Notes on the Theory of Organisation*, in Gulick, Luther; Urwick, Lyndall (eds.). *Papers on the Science of Administration*. New York 1937.

Kirkman R./Moore T., *The Walking Dead #6*, Orange 2004.

Knoster T., *A framework for thinking about systems change* in Villa, R. and Thousand, J. (eds.) *Restructuring for Caring and Effective Education: Piecing the Puzzle Together*, pp. 93–128. Baltimore 2003.

Kübler-Ross E., *On Death and Dying: What the Dying Have to Teach Doctors, Nurses, Clergy and Their Own Families*, New York 1969.

Maslow A., *Hierarchy of Needs: A Theory of Human Motivation*, Eastford 2013.

Mehrabian A., *Nonverbal Communication*, London 2007.

Nelson P., *The Joy of Money - The guide to women's financial freedom*, New York 1975.

McCrindle M./Buckwerfield S., *Generation Alpha*, Sydney 2021.

McCrindle M./Wolfinger E., *The ABC of XYZ: Understanding the Global Generations*, Sydney 2010.

OECD.org, *Free Trade Zones are being used to counterfeit goods*, in Newsroom 13.08.2018, www.oecd.org/newsroom/free-trade-zones-are-being-used-to-traffic-counterfeit-goods.htm.

Peters T./Waterman Jr. R., *In search of Excellence*, New York 2012.

Sammons S., *Linked to Influence: 7 Powerful Rules for Becoming a Top Influencer in Your Market and Attracting Your Ideal Clients on LinkedIn*, Venice (FL) 2015.

Sinek S., *Start with why: How Great Leaders Inspire Everyone to Take Action*, London 2011.

Westphalen S-A., *Reporting on Human Capital; Objectives and Trends*, in Measuring and Reporting Intellectual Capital: Experience, Issues, and Prospects Amsterdam, OECD Technical Meeting 9-10 June 1999, www.oecd.org/sti/ind/1948014.pdf

Index

CPSIA information can be obtained
at www.ICGtesting.com
Printed in the USA
BVHW091916090721
611564BV00002B/240